A CRITICAL STUDY OF THE SELECTED PLAYS OF MAHESH DATTANI AND VIJAY TENDULKAR

A CRITICAL STUDY OF THE SELECTED PLAYS OF MAHESH DATTANI AND VIJAY TENDULKAR

Sujoy Barman

AUTHORSPRESS

Worldwide Circulation through Authorspress Global Network
First Published in 2021
by
Authorspress
Q-2A Hauz Khas Enclave, New Delhi-110 016 (India)
Phone: (0) 9818049852
E-mail: authorspressgroup@gmail.com
Website: www.authorspressbooks.com

A Critical Study of the Selected Plays of
Mahesh Dattani and Vijay Tendulkar
ISBN 978-93-91314-60-6

Printed in India at Thomson Press (India) Limited

Contents

Introduction

In literature, the drama is a major genre and it has been practiced profoundly from the ancient time, for examples the classical Greek drama and Indian Sanskrit drama. Generally, the terms 'drama' and 'play' seem to be synonyms for each other, and sometimes it seems that these terms stand for substitute for each other, and one is used as a synonym for the other. But there are some major differences between these genres in definitions and formations. Drama stands for a piece of work either in prose or verse, and it has been intended to be read, not to be performed on the stage in the presence of the audience. In short the theatre plays the silent role in drama and it may or may not be an essential part for drama. For example, Closet Drama is used to read in the closed room, and it has neither audience nor theatre, but it has only reader. The term 'play' is used in the sense of literary composition and it is composed for performance on the stage at the presence of audience. Both drama and play contain dialogues between characters, but for drama, dialogues are read, and for play, these are recited on the stage among characters. In short, when a drama is performed on the stage, it becomes a play. The first major distinction between drama and play is that one is performed and another is read. The drama has its reader, whereas the play has its audience. Drama is directly connected with its reader, who understands and analyses the spirit of drama. The reader does not depend on anybody for explanation to drama as he directly perceives it. The success of the drama depends on the dramatist and his narrative technique. On the other hand, play is enjoyed and explained by the actors for the audience. The play's success depends on the actors, their acting skills, and stage condition because through their performance; the spectators come to know the meaning of the play. Here the playwright is absent behind the success of his play. The theatre is the performing place where the actors perform in the presence of the audience. The theatre may be either inside a building or in the open sky. It contains a stage for performance and a seating area for the audience. Drama, play, and theatre are the popular functions of cultural society from ancient time across the world for every ethnic society. For example, in ancient Greek culture, the most important Greek dramatists and playwrights were Euripides, Aeschylus, Sophocles, and Aristophanes. India is also a country of cultural heritage, and the history of drama, play, and theatre in India is the oldest one, and it was probably started in 200 BCE. The origin of the classical Indian drama depended on the Vadas and mythical stories. The classical Indian drama was written in Sanskrit and Prakrit languages and performed in the temple. It was a period for the origin of the 'Temple Theatre' in the history of Indian culture. The Indian classical drama belongs to Sanskrit literature. The major figures of the Indian classical drama were Bhasa, Shudraka, Harsha, Ashwaghosh, and Kalidasa. The spirit of the classical theory of Indian theatre has been preserved in the *Natyasastra*. It contains a description of the performing art on the stage.

The history of modern Indian drama began with British colonialism in India from the eighteenth century. In the early phase, there were two trends in the history of modern Indian drama. The first trend was the writing drama under the banner of Indian clasical Sanskrit drama, and the second was adopting the English drama by the Indian dramatists. They adopted materials from ancient Sanskrit literature and as well as from English literature. The Indian dramatists imitated the Shakespearean style and the English theatre for the Indian drama. When the subject is the influence of the Sanskrit literature on the modern Indian drama, the Hindu mythology has been given the priority, the stories from Hindu Gods and Goddesses are imitated on the theatre. Modern dramatists adopt their materials from classical Indian literature and mythical society. India is a multicultural country, and it has its own several cultures and literatures. So the next important feature of the Indian drama relates with the subject of diversity, and it is divided into several local and regional dramas and plays according to dialect and its people, for example Bengali drama and theatre, Hindi drama and theatre, Marathi drama and theatre, and Telugu drama and theatre. Such divisions are made according to the impact of indigenous values on drama writing. The test of regional and locality is the third feature of modern Indian drama and theatre. The English drama in India has come to existence under English literature, and it has been divided into Pre-Independence Indian English Drama and Post-Independence Indian English Drama. The important dramatists and playwrights in India's Pre-Independence drama were Krishna Mohan, Michael Madhusudan Dutta, Sir Aurobindo Ghosh, and Rabindra Nath Tagore. The spirit of British colonialism influenced these dramatists and playwrights, and their plays contain the anti-colonial spirit. After the liberation of India, there are found modifications in the spirit of contemporary modern drama. The problems of post-colonial Indian life are performed on the stage. The major figures of this period are Nissim Ezekiel, Girish Karnad, Vijay Tendulkar, Mahesh Dattani, and Badal Sircar. Nissim Ezekiel is known for his three plays which were published in a single year, 1969. They are *Nalini: A Comedy*, *Marriage Poem: A Tragi comedy*, and *The Sleep Walkers: An Indo-American Farce*. Girish Kanrad is a writer, director, and actor, and he adopts his plays from history, mythology, and old legend. The masterpiece works by him are *Yayati* (1961), *Tughlaq* (1962), *Hay Vadana* (1970), and *Nagamandala* (1972). Badal Sircar is known for his representation of the New Theatrical Movement in India. The best works by him are *Evam Indrajit* (1962), *Basi Khabar*, and *Baki Itihaash*.

Mahesh Dattanti

For contemporary Indian drama and theatre, Mahesh Dattani's name has been sketched with golden ink in the history of modern Indian literature. He is a man of versatile qualities and has been credited for providing a new spirit to contemporary Indian theatre. He is an actor, playwright, and director of the theatre, and has established a theatre group. He was born in Bangalore in Karnataka on seventh August 1958, in a Gujarati family. The life of Mahesh Dattani from his childhood has been intermingled between South Indian culture and Gujarati culture. He took his education from Baldwin Boys High School and then from St Joseph College in Bangalore. Dattani has done his graduation in Economics, History, and Political Science, and he did his postgraduate in Marketing and Advertising Management. Mahesh Dattani has planned for his career and wanted to be a copywriter and worked with the Bangalore Little Theatre. He has debuted as an actor in the play, *Surya Shikar*, by Utpal Dutta, an Indian director, playwright, and primarily known for his contribution to the Bengali Theatre. He has begun his career for theatre under the influence of Gujarati playwright Madhu Rye and English playwright Edward Albee. The year 1984 is the most important for Mahesh Dattani as he established his own theatre group 'Playpen.' In 1986, he wrote his first full-length play, *Where There's a Will*. He has been credited as the first English language playwright to have won the Sahitya Akademi award for his book, *Final Solution and Other Plays* in 1998, published by East-West Books in Chennai. Mahesh Dattani is one of the twenty-one chosen writers by BBC to write radio plays to commemorate Geoffrey Chaucer's 600th anniversary in 2000. He teaches theatre courses at the Summer Sessions Programme of Portland State University, Oregon, USA. At present, Mahesh Dattani is living in Bangalore. Most of his plays have been adopted in movies, and he also directed these movies. In 2002 Mahesh Dattani directed his play *Mango Souffle*. His *Dance Like a Man* was adopted in a movie in 2003, and Pamela Rook directed it. It was awarded with the title of 'Best Picture in English' at the National Panorama. In 2004 Mahesh Dattani wrote and directed his *Morning Raga*, and it was also awarded with the 'Best Artistic Contribution' at the Cairo Film Festival.

Mahesh Dattani is famous for creating some renounced titles in the history of contemporary Indian drama. These titles are *Seven Steps Around the Fire*, *Final Solutions*, *Bravely Fought the Queen*, *Dance Like a Man*, *Do the Needful*, *On a Muggy Night in Mumbai*, and *Tara*. He is a socialist in writing, and through his dramas and theatrical performances, Mahesh Dattani very artistically treats society and its faults. The basic spirit of his writing is socialism. Dattani is renounced for his treatment of domestic relationships and the common problems in the urban life which are common in contemporary India. He criticizes family relations based on gender discrimination, and has pointed out the issues for the domestic violence. In *Tara*, he criticizes the discriminated outlooks of parents for their children based on gender, and the injustices of parents of their children. It is natural in the Hindu patriarch society that a son is given priority rather than a daughter, and a son is preferred to a daughter. In this play, Mahesh Dattani has criticized this ideology of parents, and the titled character of the play stands for all those daughters, who are neglected by their parents. In another play, *Bravely Fought the Queen*, Mahesh Dattani has portrayed the harsh reality of the relation between husband and wife. Dolly and Lata represent all the domestic wives who are puppets at hand for their husbands. In this play, Dattani shows how the wives have been dominated and marginalized in the family by their husbands and the masculine authority. The conflict between gender and tradition is also presented in the play, *Dance Like a Man*. In India, dance is regarded as a feminine art, and the practice of dance by a man is harshly criticized in the Indian traditional society. Jairaj is a passionate male dancer, and the harmony of his life has been destroyed for his passion for the feminine art form, dance. The play shows that a male never is accepted in the female world, whereas a female is accepted in the male world. Mahesh Dattani is profoundly read for his outlook on gender discrimination and his voice for women's empowerment both in family and in society. He has also pointed out inequality power distribution among the family members based on gender. In short, gender discrimination is one of the primary themes of Mahesh Dattani's plays after the domestic disharmony. In *Seven Steps Around the Fire*, Mahesh Dattani presents the plight of the third gender in the patriarchal society. It is a play where Dattani shows an existential crisis of the eunuch community in India. They have no proper political rights, and they are looked as the queer objects in society for their gender. Kamala is a eunuch and murdered, but Mahesh Dattani mocks at the muteness of authority and civil society in this play. Everyone knows the culprit, but nobody dares to raise a voice against this injustice and punish the culprit.

Mahesh Dattani has been credited for his excellent use of theatre. He has introduced a new technique to the setting of the theatre. He has divided the theatre into several sections, and throughout the play, every section plays an important role to motivate the main action. In this regard, the stage light plays the most significant role because it divides the theatre into different sections. These sections are used to indicate different places and times. In short, for such a technique of theatrical division, Mahesh Dattani enables to present multiple settings at a time to the audience. The next important quality of Mahesh Dattani as a playwright is his creation of powerful backstage characters, these characters never appear on the stage for performance, but they, behind the stage control the play's main action, and they control the actions of other characters. Kamala does not come on the stage, and her murder never is seen in the play, *Seven Steps Around the Fire*. The play commences after the murder of Kamala. But from the beginning to the conclusion, she and her murder dominate all the characters and their performances. For her Ph.D. thesis, Uma selects Kamala and her murder as the research samples, and through her data collections for her thesis, she has discovered the main plot of the play. Praful is another powerful backstage character in the play, *Bravely Fought the Queen*. Like the eunuch Kamala, he never appears on the stage, but he dominates the Trivedi brothers and his sisters throughout the play.

Vijay Dhondopant Tendulkar
1928-2008

Vijay Dhondopant Tendulkar is a renounced name in the modern history of Marathi theatre and also in the modern Indian theatre. He wrote basically for the Marathi theatre, but his plays have been translated and performed in many Indian languages. His plays are regarded as the classics of Marathi literature. Vijay Tendulkar is a theatre thespian from Maharashtra. He was a playwright, television writer, and social commentator. Vijay Tendulkar was born in 1928 in the British Bombay Presidency (now is called Mumbai). He belonged to an artistic and cultural family. His father was a playwright, theatre artist, and he ran a small publishing house. It was his father who motivated child Vijay Tendulkar for playwriting. He was an excellent child, and from his very childhood, he began playwriting. It is said that Vijay Tendulkar wrote his first play when he was eleven years old. He spent his time in three different cities – Bombay, Pune, and Kolhapur. Tendulkar worked for the daily Navbharat. In the 1940s, he participated in the Indian liberation movement, and was a follower of Mahatma Gandhi. Vijay Tendulkar became a renounced playwright after the liberation of India in 1947. In 1955 he finished his first noted play, *Household* (*Gruhasta*). But he created a powerhouse position in the Marathi theatre in the succeeding years for his three masterpiece plays. These plays are *Silence! The Court is in Session* (*Shantata! Court Chalu Aahe*, 1967), *Sakharam Binder* (1972); and *Ghashiram Kotwal* (1972). Vijay Tendulkar, throughout his life, won some prestigious awards. In 1984 he was awarded with the title Padma Bhushan, and in 1990

Tendulkar was crowned with the title Maharashtra Gourav Puraskar Award. He was also awarded the Vishnudas Bhave Memorial Award and the Katha Chudamani Award for successfully raising social issues through his plays. The year 2002 was the most pathetic in his life because he has lost his dearest daughter, Priya Tendulkar, a renounced TV actress. Vijay Tendulkar passed on the nineteenth of May 2008.

Vijay Tendulkar is credited for his criticism of society on the stage in the presence of the audience. He is titled as the commentator of society because he very craftily criticizes the dogmatic ideas that are the main reasons for disharmony in a society. He has pointed out the prejudious perspective of the Indian civil society for the tribal people. In the play, *Kamala*, Vijay Tendulkar harshly criticizes the contemporary educated society for its negligence towards a tribal woman. In this play, a tribal woman is devaluated by the civil society where her innocence and simplicity of life have been butchered with the complexity of modernism. But in the play, *Kanyadaan*, Vijay Tendulkar has presented an adverse picture. Here the civilized society has been defeated at the hand of the uncivilized culture of tribal society. Nath, his daughter, Jyoti, and his family are mentally tortured by a tribal man, Arun. The next important feature of the plays of Vijay Tendulkar is the women's empowerment. In contemporary society, women's position is a burning issue, and Vijay Tendulkar has pointed it out in his plays. In *Silence! The Court is in Session*, Tendulkar shows how the patriarch society dominates the females under the consideration of majority and minority. Here Tendulkar show the problem of women who are determined as minor. It is a play within a play, and here Miss Leela Benera has been trapped by her colleagues of a drama troop who perform a play on the personal life of Miss Leela Benare under the consideration of a rehearsal for the final show. *Ghashiram Kotwal* is a historical play by Vijay Tendulkar, and he sets this play in eighteenth-century India. It shows the end of the Peshwa rule in Pune. Nana Phadnavis is the ruler of Pune in this play, and he is depicted as a womanizer who exploits his power. It has been pointed out that Vijay Tendulkar wrote this play on the contemporary political situation. It was a reaction to the rise of the power of Shiv Sena in Maharashtra. *A Friend's Story* is a homosexual play by Vijay Tendulkar. Here he proves his innovative ideas in writing as he wrote a play on such a theme which did not explain frankly during this time. It was the earliest piece of work in the history of the homosexual study.

Mahesh Dattani

1

Seven Steps around the Fire

The *Seven Steps Around the Fire* is a radio play, and it was first broadcasted by BBC Radio 4 on ninth January 1999 under the title, *Seven Circles Around the Fire*. The play takes its setting in the city of Bangalore, and through this play, Mahesh Dattani explains the plight of the third gender community in the modern Indian Hindu Society. It is a play about social discrimination for the hijra or eunuch community, and their exclusion from the mainstream of society according to their gender background. Mahesh Dattani has highlighted the post-independent Indian society and its problems. India has liberated from the clutches of British colonialism, and it has entered to the modern world, but the country is still under the domination of the dogmatic ideas of living. The country is modernized under the western philosophy, but it has failed to liberate the country form some traditional doctrinaires. The *Seven Steps Around the Fire* is known for its proficient treatment to its themes like the situation of the eunuch community in the twentieth century India. It is a play on the question of queer people in society. It is also a detective play where Uma Rao probes the mysterious murder of a eunuch, Kamal. Here Mahesh Dattani also presents the spirit of the Indian higher education system. The play takes an academic field for the its setting. An Indian research scholar, working on her thesis on gender discrimination and the plight of the third gender people in the Indian Hindu patriarch society is the mouthspeaker of the dramatist, Mahesh Dattani. As a playwright, Mahesh Dattani has not followed the classical trends of the playwriting for his play, *Seven Steps Around the Fire*. He divided the play into several minor scenes rather than Acts and big scenes like the classical authors. He is known for his innovative techniques for drama.

Summary

The play opens in the office of the Superintendent of Police in Bangalore, and Suresh Rao is the superintendent of this station. His wife, Uma Rao, is a research scholar and she visits to her husband's office to collect some research materials for her thesis on the subject of gender related violence in the society. Uma is also a teacher of sociology at the University of Bangalore. She belongs to the elite Hindu society, and her father is the Vice-Chancellor, and her father-in-law is the Deputy Commissioner of Police. She visits her husband's office to have an interview with Anarkali who is a eunuch. The motive of this meeting is to gather information for her thesis. Anarkali has been arrested on the charge of murder of a fellow eunuch or hijra, Kamala. Here Mahesh Dattani opens the play after the murder of Kamala, and the action of the play is to probe to solve the mystery of the murder through his mouthpiece character, Uma Rao, who takes Anarkali and the mystery of Kamala's murder as the research samples for her. It is her husband who permits Uma to meet Anarkali so that she can collect her data. It is not a normal incident that a woman from the elite Hindu society visits police station, as it is considered as a degraded act in the society. Munswamy is the constable who assists Uma, when she talks with Anarkali. For Munswamy, it is a shocking incident that an elite lady shows her interest for a eunuch who is considered as the sign of black spot in the society. He can't take it casually. So Munswamy suggests Uma not to show any interest in Anarkali, and requests her to take other cases as her research sample rather than Anarkali. He suggests her to take a male prisoner who has cut off his wife's nose. In this play Mahesh Dattani uses minor scenes rather that big acts and scenes, and the action of the play moves from one scene from another very artistically. From the office of Suresh Rao the action moves to the male section of the central jail where Anarkali is imprisoned with male prisoners. Anarkali is a hijra, and she is put in a cell with male prisoners. Here Dattani shows the big fault of the administrative system that the eunuchs are regarded as the third gender, but for them, there is no separate cell in the prisons whereas there are separated cells for men and women prisoners. Here fellow male prisoners of Anarakli beat her, and Uma on the other hand, cries out to stop the beating. Anarkali shows no interest in talking with Uma and Munswamy. The scene of the play moves to the bedroom of Uma and Suresh Rao. A TV is on, and a fight scene from a Hindi movie is blaring. In the next room, Uma talks about Anarkali with her husband, Suresh, and Uma talks about the corrupted system for putting Anarkali in a male cell as the system fails to provide a separate cell to a eunuch. For this system, the lives of hijras in prisons become critical as the male prisoners beat them. Suresh asks his wife, Uma, not to believe Anarkali, as it is a general conscious of people that eunuchs are liars, and as Anarkali is a eunuch, she must tell some imaginary stories to Uma. Mahesh Dattani criticises the society for such traditional doctrines about the eunuch. In this society, they are castrated and degenerated objects, and they fight like dogs every day. Here through Uma Rao, Mahesh Dattani provides a mythical definition to the concept of hijra. The term hijra is derived from Urdu, and it means neither male nor female. According to the Hindu mythical story, when Lord Rama was going to cross the river at the time of his exile in the forest, all people of the city wanted to follow him, and he ordered to turn back to all men and women. But some male followers wanted to follow Rama, and they did not know what to do. In such conditions, they could not disobey him, and so they sacrificed their masculinity to become neither men nor women, and they followed Lord Rama in the forest. It is the mythical incident behind the origin of the hijra community in the Hindu society. In most cases, it is noticed in this play Mahesh Dattani addresses Anarkali with the pronoun 'it' rather than the pronouns 'he' or 'she'.

In this play, the action takes place from one scene to another very sharply. Now the scene is shifted in the office of the superintendent of police, and once again, Uma comes to her husband's office to meet Anarkali to collect information about her thesis on the gender related violence. From Anarkali, Uma comes to know the tradition of the eunuch society where the spiritual relation is given priority rather than the other. The eye contact is the system by which the relation has been established. Anarkali is asking for a cigarette to smoke, and Uma provides her husband's cigarette. She also sends Munswamy to buy a new packet of cigarettes to replace the used one. Uma informs Anarkali about herself and her interest in talking with her. She is a teacher at the University of Bangalore in the depearment of sociology, and doing her thesis on class and gender-related violence. To complete her thesis, Uma has come to collect information from her. Anarkali provides her information about their daily life of singing and dancing at weddings and birthday parties, and their collections from these functions. They always either blesses or curses to the people surrounded them. Then both are talking about the subject of sisterhood in the eunuch society. Through their conversation, Anarkali repeats that she is not the murder of Kamala, and asks Uma to arrange her release from the prison by exercising her family background as she is the daughter-in-law of the Deputy Commissioner of Police. Anarkali knows the culprit behind the murder of her sister, Kamala, but she can't tell the truth to Uma as she is conscious that Uma can't help her because the murder is a very powerful man. On the other hand, Uma also assures her that she does not want to involve in this situation and shows her reluctance to help her in this regard as she is only collecting the information for her thesis. But later, Uma shows her interest in releasing Anarkali from the imprisonment. She directs Uma to meet Champa, the head of hijras, who will arrange her release from the imprisonment if she has money. Champa lives behind Russel Market in Shivajinagar. Their conversation is interrupted at the arrival of Munswamy with a packet of cigarettes. The meeting with Anarkali is finished after the arrival of Suresh Rao, and he directs Munswamy to assist his wife, Uma, to the house of his father-in-law.

The action of the play shifts from the office of Suresh Rao to street. The road is busy, and Uma and Munswamy are inside the car, and waiting for the traffic signal. Here Mahesh Dattani presents a true picture of the Indian roads where the beggars including children are buzzing, and the passengers are avoiding their presence. Munswamy informs Uma of the recovery to the dead body of Kamala that was abandoned in a pond after being burned. The eunuch didn't complain about the missing of Kamala, and when the dead body was found, they were interested in the jewellery of Kamala. They didn't mourn at the death of their sister, Kamala. Munswamy informs Uma about the increasing crime rate in society, and most of the criminals belong to the lower and beggar society. He suggests Uma to keep distance from the street beggars as they are recognized to have a criminal background. From the car, Uma throws coins for the beggar's children.

Both Uma and Munswamy reach the house of Uma's father, but her father is absent, and Uma makes a call to her father in the office of the Vice-Chancellor. Uma asks for money, about fifty thousand for the wedding gift for Mr. Sharma's son, Subramanyan or Subbu. He is a minister and in this play is standing as the patriarch figure. She gets in the car and asks Munswamy to take the car to Shivajinagar. It is a red-lighted area, and people from the higher class avoid this area generally. Munswamy is shocked, and he switches off the car's engine. Uma intends to meet Champa, the head of the hijras, and she gets out of the car and hires a rickshaw. Constable Munswamy reluctantly assists Uma to the house of Champa. The next scene of the play is the living room of Champa, who at first guesses Uma as a journalist, but Uma assures that she is not a journalist. Champa also guesses that Uma perhaps has come there searching for her son, and she informs her that they have not kidnapped her son. But Uma identifies herself as a social worker, and she has come according to the guidance of Anarkali. Through their conversation, Champa asks Uma not to help Anarkali at first, but Champa wants to release Anarkali. Champa is the guru of the eunuch society, and her first choice was Kamala to be the next guru after her retirement. As Kamala is murdered and it becomes clear that Anarkali will be the next guru of the eunuch community after Champa's retirement. Champa realizes that Uma has come with money to help Anarkali; because of lack of money, Champa cannot release Anarkali from jail. In the conversation, it becomes clear that Anarkali has not killed Kamala. Their conversation is interrupted at the sudden arrival of Salim, the body-gourd of Minister Sharma. They hide the bundle of the money. Salim comes in search of Kamala's possession, and he is looking for Kamala's trunk. When Salim comes to know the identification of Uma as the daughter-in-law of Deputy Commissioner of Police, he leaves Champa's apartment. After Salim's departure, Uma asks about Salim and his searching. Champa informs her that Salim is searching for a photograph, and he is the bodyguard of the Minister who lives in the Palace Orchards. Champa shows Uma the trunk of Kamala, and Uma notices a beautiful portrait of Kamala. The interest of Uma to the mystery of Kamala's murder increases. She takes the case very seriously after Salim's visit to Champa. She asks Champa about the reason for Salim's visit but does not gain pertinent information from Champa. Then Uma, with constable Munswamy, moves to the Minister's house to meet Salim to find out some information behind the mystery of Kamala's murder. They cross the gate of the Minister's house, and Uma asks Salim about his wife with whom she wants to talk. But Salim informs her that his wife has gone to the village. Uma also asks about Subbu, the son of the Minister, and this question frightens Salim. At this time, Minister Mr. Sharma comes on the stage, and his appearance creates a puzzling situation for Uma and Munswamy. Uma introduces herself with Mr. Sharma and tells him the reasons behind her visit to his house. Uma guesses that Salim and his wife are the culprits behind the murder of Kamala, but Mr. Sharma presents an adverse view, and he assures Uma that other hijras have murdered Kamala. Then Subbu comes on the scene, and he leads a traumatic life about his upcoming wedding. Subbu requests Uma not to arrest Salim as he is innocent. Here Subbu gives some clues to Uma for the mysterious death of Kamala.

The action of the play shifts to the bedroom of Suresh and Uma. Both are taking tea, and discussing about the wedding gift for Subbu. Suresh informs Uma that her father called him, and asks about the money which Uma received from her father. She takes it for the bail of Anarkali but Uma hides it, and says that she has taken money to buy a wedding gift for Subbu. They are also talking about their marital life without children. Uma has visited a doctor to test her pregnancy. Then Suresh asks about the progress of her thesis, and Uma is also informed that Anarkali has been released from jail. The scene of the play moves from the bedroom of Uma to the house of Champa in the Bazaar. After knowing the news about the release of Anarkali, Uma visits the house of Champa to meet Anarkali. Here she comes to know about the photograph that Salim wanted badly. Champa informs Uma that it is not Salim who killed Kamala, there is other dangerous figure behind this murder, and Salim is only a puppet for him. Uma meets Anarkali, who has been beaten bitterly in prison. They are talking about the wedding of Subbu, son of Minister Sharma. The next scene of the play is the wedding of Subbu. The house of Minister Mr. Sharma is full of guests, and Uma with her husband, Suresh, attends the wedding. Both Uma and Mr. Sharma indulge in conversations about the mysterious murder of Kamala. Subbu is getting a wife from an elite family. Uma goes to the servant's quarters to meet Salim's wife. But Salim assures her that his wife knows nothing. In the meantime, Champa, Anarkali, and other hijras enter the wedding ceremony. But they are rebuked by Minister Mr. Sharma, who wants to get rid of them from the ceremony, but Uma comes ahead and defends it. She says that it will be an unfortunate incident if they are rid of the wedding. The arrival of the hijras in the wedding gives light on the main plot of the play. It becomes clear that Subbu has a relation with Kamala and both are secretly married. At the wedding, Anarkali shows Subbu the photograph that Salim badly searched for. In an abnormal condition, Subbu kills himself with a gun. After the suicide of Subbu, the action of the play takes place in the living room of Champa, where Uma visits to meet Anarkali. She comes to know that Champa has retired from the post of the guru, and it is now Anarkali who becomes the new guru. Anarkali provides all information behind the murder of Kamala. She tells her that Kamala loved Subbu and both secretly married which was not accepted in the society, so some hired ruffians abducted Kamala and killed her. Anarkali prevented Kamala from making relation with Subbu as she is very conscious with the system in the society, and she disfigured her face so that Subbu hated her, but her attempt did not work, and they continued their relation. At the end of the play, Mahesh Dattani gives light to the photograph. It is a Polaroid picture that Subbu and Kamala had taken soon after their private wedding in a remote temple. The play ends with certain questions, and there are some uncertain answers to these certain questions. Anarkali, Champa, all hijra, and other people know who is behind the murder of Kamala, but nobody dares to say against this crime and its culprit. Here Dattani presents the muteness of society against the injustice of eunuch community. It is a play about the disability of the eunuch community. The newspapers hide the real incident, and the police made no arrest, and Subbu's suicide has been written off as an accident in the newspapers. Champa was right that nobody will be arrested. The photograph has been destroyed. The play concludes with the question of the right of eunuch community in the society. It also indicates the spiritual union of Kamala and Subbu after their deaths where the social barriers are far away from their love.

The Critical Appreciation of the Play

Title

The play, *Seven Steps Around the Fire*, is a short but very complicated play according to its socio-political background. It is a play that highlights on dark sides of the Indian Hindu patriarch society, and the play is also a voice for the rights of the eunuch and hijra people in society. It is a play for their political and social rights. The play, *Seven Steps Around the Fire*, attacks the dogmatic ideas of the Hindu society on the subject of gender. In the Hindu wedding, the phrase 'Seven Steps' stands for a ritual, and without it, the wedding remains incomplete. It stands for seven pheras or seven vows which bride and bridegroom have to take. In this ritual, the bride and bridegroom take seven vows for each other through their seven steps around the fire. These steps stand for nourishment, strength, prosper and faithful, love and respect, care for children, healthy and peaceful life, and lastly friendship and loyalty for a happy marital life. In this play, *Seven Steps Around the Fire*, these seven vows are taken between Kamala and Subbu. But their marriage is not accepted in society, and after the marriage, Kamala is murdered by the father of Subbu, and the play ends with the suicide of Subbu. The play's title is apt and appropriate, and after the death of Kamala, Subbu never forgets his vows to Kamala, and he denies his second marriage. He is a faithful to his partner, Kamala, and at the end of the play, Subbu kills himself to meet Kamala after death. Thus the dignity of seven vows in the play is maintained by Subbu.

Technique

Mahesh Dattani uses a typical style for narrating the story of his play. He is an innovative playwright in the history of Indian drama and theatre. Dattani is praised for his unique technique. He knows how to utilize the theatre for a perfect presentation. Mahesh Dattani used a typical technique for presenting his play, *Seven Steps Around the Fire*, on the stage. He has used several minor scenes rather than the Acts and big Scenes like the classical plays. The action takes place in the office of the Superintendent of Police, in the car, in the bedroom of Uma and Suresh Rao, in Champa's living room, and in the house of Minister Mr Sharma. The play's action moves from one place to another, and Mahesh Dattani has proved his craftsmanship for the sharp moving of the action from one scene to another.

Queer Element

Thematically the play is on the subject of queer. The eunuch community is regarded as the queer in the Hindu society, and here, Dattani portrays these people's lives, and talks about their socio-political rights. The term 'Queer' refers to those subjects, which are regarded as abnormal, odd, and strange from the conventional perspective. The term is profoundly used in the gender study and refers to gay and lesbian people. Gay, lesbian, bisexual, and transsexual are the major subjects in queer study. Michel Foucault is the main exponent of the queer theory in the history of theory and criticism. In Indian society, the hijra society and eunuchs are considered as queers, and they are discriminated against in the society for their queer background. The play is a criticism to the system, and Dattani talks about the empowerment to the eunuch community. The hijra people are sub-categorized in society for their gender background. They are identified as criminals and thought to perform criminal acts like kidnapping children. As they belong to the third gender, they possess the third position in society. The hijra community stands after men and women in society, providing poor socio-political rights in society. At the beginning of the play, Anarkali is imprisoned for the murder of a fellow hijra, Kamala, without a proper investigation to the murder. But in prison, she is not provided a separate cell, and she is put in a cell with male prisoners rather than the female prisoners. Anarkali belongs to the third gender, and she is put in a cell with first gender prisoners, where fellow male prisoners beat her. At the same time, the people like Suresh Rao in society call hijra by using the pronoun "it" rather than "he" or "she." This marks the cruel existential condition of the hijra in the Indian society.

Murder Mystery Play

The play, *Seven Steps Around the Fire*, is a murder mystery play, and it centers on the murder of a eunuch, Kamala. All the actions of this play are motivated by the incident of the mysterious murder of Kamala. It opens after the murder of Kamala and it concludes with another death of Subbu Sharma. Throughout the play, Uma probes the murder of Kamala. Society knows the culprit behind this murder, but everyone is silent against this crime. The police authority, media, and even the hijra people do not dare to punish the culprit Minister Mr Sharma. Uma Rao, a teacher and researcher brings light on this crime through her collection of research samples for her thesis on gender-related violence in society. Uma, in this play, performs her role as a detective to solve the murder mystery.

Higher Education System

The play, *Seven Steps Around the Fire*, sets on the higher education system in post-independent India. A trend in the contemporary research field in the Indian higher academic section is to select some sociological issues as the research area. Here Uma Rao, as a research scholar, selects the hijra society as her research area. She writes her thesis on the topic of violence in society for the hijra people. The eunuch, Anarkali, and the murder mystery of Kamala are the research samples for the thesis. She possesses an interrogating spirit that enables her to move towards the truth of Kamala's murder. Here Mahesh Dattani, in this play, has used a typical narrative technique. Generally, the play is about Uma and her collection of data's for the thesis on gender-related violence in society. From beginning to end, the plot of the play deals with Uma and her collection of datas for her thesis with the help of her husband, Suresh Rao, and constable, Munswamy. But actually, main action is based on the murder of Kamala and the injustice for the hijra people in society. Mahesh Dattani's narrative technique conveys two similar meanings. The first meaning relates to Uma Rao and her thesis, whereas the second meaning deals with the murder of Kamala and injustice in the society for the hijra people.

Characters

Kamala

Kamala is the central character of the play. She does not appear on the stage physically, but her presence is noticed on every character, and in every action throughout the play. She plays her role behind the stage and dominates all. The plays open after her murder, and throughout the play, Uma is searching for the motives of her murder, and the play concludes with the determination of the murder mystery. She is a eunuch, and she secretly married the Minister's son, Subbhu Sharma. The title of the play, *Seven Steps Around the Fire*, indicates the marriage between Kamala and Subbu Sharma. But this marriage has caused the premature death of Kamala. Uma Rao selects this murder as the research sample of her thesis, and through her, Kamala is presented in this play.

Uma Rao

Uma Rao is the next important character of the play, *Seven Steps Around the Fire*. She is the mouth speaker of Mahesh Dattani. She is a teacher at the University of Bangalore in department of sociology, and at present, she is pursuing her thesis on gender-related violence in society. Uma belongs to the elite society. She is the daughter of the vice-chancellor, the wife of the Superintendent of Police, and her father-in-law is the Deputy Commissioner of Police. To complete her thesis on gender-related violence in society, Uma Rao selects Anarkali and the mysterious murder of Kamala as her research samples. In the play, she becomes the mouth-speaker Mahesh Dattani, and through her, the playwright presents his points of view. Uma Rao manages money for Anarkali's bail. She is a bold character. To gather information, she visits Champ's house and follows Salim to the house of Minister Mr. Sharma. Generally, the ladies from the elite society avoid the hijra society, but here Uma pays visits to Champa, the head and guru of hijra society. Uma knows that her sudden visit to the Minister's house to follow Salim may create her problem, yet she is bold to visit Minister Mr. Sharma's house.

Anarkali

Anarkali is a eunuch in the play, *Seven Steps Around the Fire*. She is the sister of Kamala and also becomes a sister to Uma Rao. At the beginning of the play, Anarkali is imprisoned on the charge of the murder of Kamala. In prison, she is beaten by her fellow male prisoners. Uma visits her to collect her research information for her thesis on gender-related violence in society. She is very conscious of the system, and she warns Kamala not to establish relationship with Subbu, the son of Minister Mr. Sharma. Anarkali witnessed the secret marriage of Kamala and Subbu, and she also knows the culprit of Kamala's murder. With the help of Uma, she has been released from the prison, and she also provides sufficient information to complete her thesis. She provides valuable information about the death of Kamala to Uma. At the end of the play, Anarkali becomes the head of the hijra community after the retirement of Champa.

Champa

Champa is the head of the hijra society who lives in Shivajinagar. She looks after the possession of Kamala after her death. She is visited by Uma, who gives money for Anarkali's bail from imprisonment. Kamala is the first choice of Champa to be the next guru for hijra community after her retirement. But for the tragic death of Kamala, Anarkali becomes the next guru after Champa's retirement.

Mr. Sharma and Subbu

Mr Sharma is the Minister in the play. He is the representative of the patriarch society. Mr Sharma kills the eunuch Kamala as he can't take Kamala as his daughter-in-law. Subbu is the only son of Mr. Sharma. Subbu loves Kamala, a beautiful hijra, and Kamala and Subbu secretly married in a remote temple. This incident is never accepted in the elite Hindu society, and such incident is considered the darkest hole for a family. To hide the secret marriage of his son with a hijra, Mr Sharma kills Kamala, and puts charges on Anarkali as the murder. Mr Sharma also arranges a marriage for his son with a lady from a well-recognized family. But Subbu is an honest partner of Kamala, and he does not accept the death of Kamala. At the end of the play, at his second wedding, Subbu kills himself. His death is relevant with the meaning of the title's phrase. According to Hindu mythology, the ritual of seven steps is a part of marriage where both bride and groom take seven holly vows for each other to lead a happy marital life. Trusty and honesty are among these seven vows. Through the suicide, Subbu proves his loyalty to his Kamala. It is Minister Mr. Sharma, and his society is responsible for the death of Kamala and Subbu.

Munswamy

Munswamy is the constable in the office of the Superintendent of Police. He is given an order by Suresh Rao, the superintendent of police, to assist his wife Uma Rao in collecting research datas for her thesis on gender-related violence in society. Munswamy assists Uma when she meets Anarkali in prison, to the market of Shivajinagar when Uma goes to meet Champa, and to the house of the Minister. Munswamy is unsatisfied with Uma's thesis and asks her to take another subject for her research rather than the Anarkali.

Salim

Salim is the bodyguard to the Minister, Mr Sharma. According to the order of Minister, he goes to the Champ's house to fetch a photograph of Kamala. Uma charges Salim and his wife as the murderers of Kamala. Salim is a good servant to his master, and he always takes orders from his master Mr. Sharma.

2

Final Solutions

The *Final Solutions* is one of the best plays of Mahesh Dattani. It is the titled play of the book that won the prestigious award, the Sahitya Academy, in 1998. The play was first performed at Guru Nanak Bhavan, Bangalore, on 10th July 1993. The play is based on the subject of communal riot between Hindu and Muslims in the post-independent India. In this play, Mahesh Dattani attempts to show some solutions to stop the riot though it seems that there is no solution to stop communal riot in India. The *Final Solutions* is a play about the three generations of a Gandhi family, and their different relations with Muslim society. Mahesh Dattani is a skilled theatre artist, and here he has very craftily used the theatre to present his play, *Final Solutions.* Most of the action of this play takes in the house of Ramnik Gandhi and in the street. The play is divided into three acts, and Mahesh Dattani here mingles past and present incidents, and the sequence of the play moves from past to present, and then present to past. It is Daksha and her diary through whom the audience is migrated to the past from the present.

Summary

Act I

The setting of the play is the house of Ramnik Gandhi in Amargaon, and it is night. The play opens with Daksha or Hardika, and she reads out her diary. She reminds her past and moves to her past life. Daksha reads the date of 31st March 1948 from her diary, when India has just received its liberty from the clutches of British colonialism. From her diary, we learn about her youth, her passion for music, and her dream to be a singer like Noor Jehan. Daksha was married to Hari, who belonged to a traditional Hindu family where the music for women was regarded as uncultured. Once Daksha was caught singing a romantic song for her husband, Hari, by her in-laws, and later, her in-laws told Hari to stop her singing. Thus the marriage shattered her dream to be a singer. The diary of Daksha is important both personally and in history. The diary provides information about the youth of Daksha, and presents the political situation of then society. In 1948 India faced the darkest period in history. The liberty and freedom brought riot for India. Through the diary, the audience realizes that the father of Daksha was a freedom fighter, and he was killed in Hussainabad by a Muslim mob. The Muslim mob also attacked the house of Daksha in the absence of her father, and in this attack, she lost all her collection of music of Shamshad Begum, Noor Jehan, and Suraiya. The gramophone was also broken in this attack. Through the diary of Daksha, Mahesh Dattani describes the political problem regarding harmony and unity of the newly liberated country, India. The riot in India has been originated with the partition and it is still presence after forty years of partition. The time changes, but the situation is not changed for the Hindu and Muslim communities. The communal riot is still a big threat for the harmony and integrity of the country. In the present time, the Rath Yatra is attacked by a Muslim mob, and the priest (poojari) has been stabbed to death by the mob. Here Dattani very craftily uses the chorus to present the Hindu mob and the Muslim mob. The chorus comprises five men, and there are five Hindu masks and five Muslim masks to perform as the Hindu mob and Muslim mob. The Hindu mob informs the attack on the Rath Yatra when it enters Kareem Bagh after Shanti Road and Nehru Gardens. The Kareem Bagh is the residential area of the Muslim community, and here the trouble begins. The light of the stage falls on the house of Ramnik Gandhi. Ramnik switches off the television, and his daughter, Smita, is talking over the phone to the parents of her Muslim friend, Tasneem, who lives in a girl's hostel. A violated Hindu mob has attacked to this hostel, and she consoles them about the safety of her friend. She assures the family that their daughter is safe. Tasneem's family is living in Jeevnagar. Ramnik takes the phone from his daughter and talks to Noor Ahmed about the safety of their daughter, Tasneem. Here Mahesh Dattani has used a zigzag narrative technique. The chorus appears as either the Hindu mob or the Muslim mob, and through Daksha, the technique back to forty years before. After the conversation between father and daughter, the stage light falls on a Muslim mob and it denies the charging of the attacking to the Rath Yatra. The stage light falls on Daksha, and she reminds her deep friendship with a Khoja woman, Zarine. The play's action then moves to the street, near the house of Ramnik Gandhi, where two Muslim men, Javed and Bobby, are chased by a Hindu mob, and they run towards the house of Ramnik Gandhi, and request him to open the door and to save from the Hindu mob. Finally, Ramnik opens the door, and they enter the house. Outside the house, the Hindu mob rebukes Ramnik for providing shelter to these Muslim men, and asks him to hand them over. But Ramnik does not pay any attention to the appcal of the Hindu mob. Here Ramnik becomes a champion of riot. But on the other hand, the arrival of two Muslim men in a traditional Hindu family during the communal riot is a traumatic incident for the ladies of the family when Hindus kill Muslims and Muslims kill Hindus. Aruna, the wife of Ramnik Gandhi, asks her husband to call the police to hand over them to the police. Through their conversation, they come to know that Bobby is from Jeevnagar, and he has just finished his college education, and Javed is dropped out of school. Ramnik asks them about the motives of their arrival in Amargaon in this riotic environment.

Act II

The setting of the stage in Act II is the same as it was in Act I. The action takes place in the house of Ramnik Gandhi. His daughter, Smita, informs her parents that she knows Javed and Bobby. Such news shocks the members of the family, especially her mother, Aruna, and grandmother, Hardika or Daksha. Smita informs them Javed is the brother of Tasneem and Booby is the fiancé of Tasneem. She knows them through her friendship with Tasneem, and she had once met Bobby when she dropped Tasneem at her hostel. Aruna asks her husband, Ramnik, to stop the college of their daughter for her friendship with Muslims. Javed is rude and bold in his conduct with the members of the Gandhi family, and he informs that he is not living with his family because his family gets him out for his friendship with corrupted people in society. During their conversation, the Hindu mob throws stones at the family, and cries out as traitors to the family for providing food and shelter to these Muslim boys. Ramnik describes the tragic incident of the Rath Yatra that has been attacked by the Muslim mob when it enters Kareem Bagh after Shanti Road and Nehru Gardens. Ramnik thinks Javed comes to Amargaon for a job, and he offers him a job in his saree shop in Kapda Bazaar. In the meantime, Smita discloses a secret of Javed's life that his family threw him out, and he has been hired by some parties to throw stones at the idol to create a riot. For this disclose, Smita is rebuked by Javed as she has betrayed her friend, Tasneem, whom she promised not to share the secret of Javed.

Act III

Act III opens with Javed, Bobby, the Muslim chorus, and Daksha, but the story moves to past from the present. The stage light fades in Daksha, and she reminds her husband, Hari, who reluctantly joined his father's clothes mill after leaving his college. Daksha also reminds her friend, Zarine, and her family. Zarine's family was in trouble during the communal riot as their fruits and mithai shop had caught fire. The family faced a financial crisis. Zarine's father went to Daksha's father-in-laws to ask for a job. But it was useless. Then the light of the stage fades on the house of Ramnik and it is the present time. Dattani as a dramatist shows his artistic quality while past and present actions are performed on the stage. Daksha and her diary are the methods to move to the past. After the description of Zarine and her family, the action of the play shifts to the present in the house of Ramnik Gandhi. Throughout the conversation, Ramnik realizes that Javed has been hired to attact Hindus. He is a part of violated Muslim mob, received thousand

and lakh rupees from the parties for attacking. Such information changes the atmosphere of the house. Ramnik is talking with a person who has attacked the Rath Yatra, and gives him selter and security in his house. Bobby defends Javed that he did such things for money but now he has changed. He indeed received money for attacking Hindu society, but he is now changed. At the same time, Bobby charges the Hindu society that forced Javed to take this way of living. He joined to the parties because once he witnessed the cruelty of the Hindu society. He is cruel and rude because he was made so. In school, Javed was a hero and smart. A minor incident changed the life of Javed. During a cricket match, Javed and other Muslim boys, including Bobby, witnessed a tragic incident that influenced the life of Javed permanently. Then the action of the play moves from present to past once again. The stage light fades on Daksha, and she reminds her visit to the house of her friend, Zarine. She comes to know that the shop of Zarine's father was intentionally burned. The shop did not accidently catch the fire, somebody put it under the fire. This information couldn't understand by Daksha. She moved to the room of Zarine and shared her experience of music in the family of her laws with Zarine. Both Zarine and Daksha played a tape of famous singer Noor Jehan in gramophone, and they also imitated the sound of the gramophone.

The action moves to present from the memory of Daksha, and the stage light fades on the living room of Ramnik Gandhi. Both Javed and Bobby are ready to leave the house as the situation outside of the house seems to be normal, and the Hindu mob has left the street. But Ramnik prevents them from leaving the house as they are parts of the Muslim mob to attack the Hindus, and he intends them to hand over the police. Ramnik also wants them to hand over to the Hindu mob. But the mob has already departed. Here Javed presents a true picture of the psychology of mob. He says the mob has left because they were not paid for over-duty. The mob is well directed where, when, and what to do by their leaders. Javed is a part of the Muslim mob, and he knows the true character of the mob. After that, Javed shares how they planned and how they attacked the Rath Yatra in Kareem Bagh. He throws stones at the chariot and kills the poojari. The conversation is interrupted by Smita and Aruna. Smita is asking for an apology to Javed as she discloses his secret to her family. The time passes, and it is a time to collect water from the tap in the street. Aruna and Smita are ready to fetch water, but Javed shows his interest in fetching water. It shocks Aruna as she is a traditional religious woman, and she always avoids the touching of Muslims. If Javed is allowed to fetch water it means that he is allowed to touch the buckets of the family. Aruna does not like that a Muslim fetches water for her family. She can't accept the idea that her god will be given birth with the water, fetched by a Muslim. In this regard Samita is open-minded and she does not believe on the idea that a Muslim can't touch the Hindu god. Both mother and daughter indulge in a debate on this subject. Smita charges her mother that she always puts her rituals and religious beliefs on her from her childhood. She has been forced to visit the temple, attend the prayer, and make garlands for god. She leads a docile life in the family, and Smita is bored with such life. She can't bear such a life. At least Smita goes outside of the house with Javed and Bobby to fetch water. The next conversation takes place among Smita, Javed, and Bobby, who are collecting water. Here it becomes clear that both Javed and Bobby have not come to the house of Smita accidentally; they have come to the house purposely. Javed wanted to make some clearness from Smita; that is why they have come to meet her. Once Bobby and Smita were very close friends, now Booby is going to marry Tasneem, sister of Javed. Javed knows this closeness between Bobby and Smita. As his sister is going to marry Bobby, Javed wants to be sure about the relation between Bobby and Smita so that his sister won't face problems in her marital life after the marriage with Booby for Smita.

All three enter the house of Ramnik Gandhi with water. The action of the play moves on Daksha and her past life. She reminds her visit to her friend Zarine and her sitting at their dinner table. For this act, Daksha was beaten by her husband, Hari. The action moves to the present and in the house of Ramnik Gandhi, where

Bobby picks the statue of Lord Krishna and then slowly and tenderly puts it in its place. Bobby says the lord Krishna does not harm him, and he says that the lack of trust is the main cause behind this critical condition. At the end of the play, Ramnik Gandhi shares their family guilt with his mother, Daksha. He says that his saree shop belonged to Zarine's father's fruits and mithai shop, and this was burnt by his father, Hari, and his grandfather in the name of communal hatred as they wanted a shop for their saree shop. This information destroys the harmony of Daksha's life as she is ignorant of it for a long time. At the same time, Ramnik feels guilty for his family and he morally too weak to enter his saree shop. The play ends with the repentance of Ramnik Gandhi and Daksha for their family's crime against the family of Zarine.

Critical Analysis of the Play

Technique

Mahesh Dattani is a skilled theatre artist, and he very craftily uses the theatre to present the action of his plays. He divides the stage into different portions for indicating different settings of the play, and the stage light plays a vital role in indicating the settings of the play. The stage for the presentation of the play, *Final Solutions*, is dominated by a horseshoe or crescent-shaped ramp, with the ends sloping to stage level. Here Dattani uses the chorus to act as either the Hindu mob or the Muslim mob throughout the play. A chorus is a classical form of the play which performs the most significant role in the presentation as it assists to the main action of the play. Dattani's chorus in this play comprises five men with ten masks on sticks. There are five Hindu masks and five Muslim masks. The chorus is the ultra-ego to the Hindu and Muslim people, and through it, Dattani attempts to say that all are supporters of communal riots or parts of it. For the presentation of the story, Mahesh Dattani used a zigzag narrative style. The past and present incidents are intermingled with each other, and it becomes difficult to understand a proper sequence of incidents throughout the play. Dattani with Daksha and her diary describes the past incidents which were taken almost forty years ago from the present time. The diary of Daksh is significant both historically and biographically. From a historical point of view, the diary describes the communal riot in India after its liberty in the year 1948. It talks about the Indian history of partition. Daksha lost her father in Hussainabad soon after the partition. This is the historical significance of Daksha's diary. The diary has its the importance of portraying the life of a young Hindu lady and her newly married life in the house of her-laws where her dreams and wishes were butchered by the tradition of the family. It presents a vivid picture of the youth of Dakaha and her married life.

Title

The title phrase "Final Solution" contains some significant meanings. Throughout the play, Mahesh Dattani attempts to provide some solutions to stop the communal riot between Hindu and Muslim communities. He considers 'trust,' 'tolerance,' and 'forgiveness' as the best solutions to stop the communal riot. Both Hindus and Muslims should trust each other. Javed is a Muslim boy who participated in the riot. He is changed, but Daksha, Ramnik, and Aruna deny that Javed has changed. The lack of trust between Hindu and Muslim communities is one of the basic reasons for the riot. The next important solution to stop the riot is 'forgiveness.' Daksha has lost her father in the communal riot at the time of partition. The Muslim mob killed her father, and for this tragic incident, she hates Muslim community, and she never forgives them. When Javed and Bobby enter the house of her son, Ramnik Gandhi, she rebukes them and charges them as the culprits of the riot. If Daksha forgives the Muslim society, and she takes Javed and Bobby normally, then there is a chance to have harmonious relation in the society. In that case, the situation may differ, and her rude behavior won't instigate others like Javed and Bobby to be involved in a riot. Thus forgiveness is a solution to stop the riot. The third solution to stop the riot is tolerance. The people should tolerate each other in society. Thus trust, forgiveness, and tolerance are the basic solutions to stop the communal riot.

Motives of Riot

In the play, *Final Solutions*, Mahesh Dattani talks about the motives of the riot, and in most cases, revenge is the major motive of the riot. One community attacks another community in revenge. The Muslims have attacked the Rath Yatra in the street of Kareem Bagh, where the poojari has been stabbed to death. To avenge this incident, the Hindu mob also attacks the Muslim girl's hostel, and two Muslim boys, Javed and Bobby. Revenge is primary motive for a riot. But the riot is controlled both by the individual benefits and by some corrupted leaders. It is profitable for some leaders who push the common public in riot for their personal benefit. For example, at the time of partition between India and Pakistan, Daksh's husband, Hari, and her father-in-law set fire to the shop of her friend, Zarine, under the name of communal riot. The actual motive of this fire was not revenge; Hari and his father wanted this shop badly to establish a saree shop. Here the personal issue plays a role behind the communal riot. The riot is the result of some corrupted-minded political and religious leaders. These leaders never appear in public, but they control the riot from home. They hire young men like Javed to create a violated mob. The corrupted leaders easily misguide young men like Javed, and they provide money for creating violence in society. Through Javed, Mahesh Dattani presents a vivid picture of the involvement of the young generation in riots under the name of religion or jihad.

Historical Play

The *Final Solutions* is a historical play based on the communal riot in the history of India. It covers the period from 1948 to 1988. In the year 1948, India faced its historical changes for partition and communal riots. With the liberation of India, the country has been divided into Pakistan (Purba or East Pakistan and Paschim or West Pakistan) and Hindustan. The time moves and but the situation has not been changed throughout the passing of the time. In 1948, Daksha's house was attacked by the Muslim mob, and her father was murdered in the street. After forty years, the situation is the same for the Hindus and Muslims. The Muslim mob has attacked the Rath Yatra, and on the other hand, the Muslim girl's hostel is also attacked by the Hindu mob. In 1948 the British government played a silent role behind the partition and communal riot; at present, some corrupted political parties and religious leaders maintain it very craftily. They hire young men like Javed to create a violated mob.

Communal Play

The *Final Solutions* is a play about three generations of a Gandhi family and their different relations with the Muslim society. The first generation belongs to Daksha. She has an intimacy with a Muslim girl, Zarine. Both love music, and Daksha visits her house, and both become good friends. But the Zarine's family has been destroyed by Daksha's husband, Hari, and her father-in-law. They set fire to the shop of Zarine's father under the name of the communal riot as they needed a shop to establish a new saree shop. The second generation belongs to Ramnik Gandhi and her wife, Aruna. Ramnik Gandhi provides food and shelter to two Muslim boys, who are chased by the Hindu mob. On the other hand, his wife is a traditional Hindu woman who always avoids Muslim presence. She thinks that her piousness will be spoiled at the presence of the Muslim. Smita Gandhi belongs to the third generation of the family, and like her grandmother, Daksha, she also has an intimate Muslim friend, Tasneem. Smita also makes friends with Javed and Bobby.

Women's Empowerment

Mahesh Dattani is known for the presentation of women characters in his plays. He presents multidimensional ways to probe the plight of women throughout his plays. In the play, *Final Solutions*, Dattani portrays the women who are dominated by politically and also by the patriarch society. Daksha has a fantasy about music in her youth, and in the traditional Hindu society, singing by women never be considered a true or reputed passion. Music is regarded as an art for the degraded people, and the higher Hindu society never allows music in their personal life. Daksha belongs to the elite society, and her in-laws dominate her passion for music. Once she has been caught to sing a romantic song for her husband, Hari, and her in-laws say Hari to stop her songs. Daksha's liberal mind is dominated by her husband, Hari, who has beaten her for sitting at the dinner table in the house of her friend, Zarine. Smita is also dominated by her family tradition. She unwillingly attends the prayers, goes to the temple, and makes garlands for god under her mother's pressure, Aruna. For the critical relation between Hindu and Muslim societies, Smita is prevented from making relations with her Muslim friends. When Aruna realizes that she knows Javed and Bobby, two Muslim boys, she asks her husband, Ramnik, to stop her education. In this play, Mahesh Dattani describes the life of Hindu women under the domination of patriarch society and by the historical incident of communal riot.

Friendship vs Hatred

Throughout the play, *Final Solutions*, Mahesh Dattani treats the theme friendship versus hatred'. He very technically shows the deep friendship between Hindu and Muslim girls, whereas these two communities kill each other in the streets. During the communal riot between Hindus and Muslims, Daksha and her granddaughter, Smita, have their strong friendship with other Muslim girls. Daksha is a friend of Zarine, and she visits her house. Both these friends are gossiping and singing. On the other hand, Daksha lost her father in a riot by the Muslims. At the same time, her husband and father-in-law set fire to the shop of Zarine's father. Thus the friendship between Daksha and Zarine has been concluded by her family. There is another example of friendship. It is between Smita and Tasneem. Both are college students. Smita is also a friend of Bobby, the lover of Tasneem. Their friendship is standing against hatred between Hindu and Muslim societies. They are friends when the Muslims attack the Rath Yatra, and the Muslim girl's hostel is attacked by the Hindus.

Characters

Daksha or Hardika

Daksha or Hardika is the oldest character in the play, *Final Solutions*. She is the mother of Ramnik Gandhi and grandmother of Smita. Zarine is her Muslim friend, and both friends love the music of Noor Jehan. Daksha has lost her father in a riot in Hussainbad, who was a freedom fighter. In her youth, she has loved Muslims, but at her old age, she hates them as she has lost her father in the riot by the Muslims. When Bobby and Javed enter the house of her son, Rmanik Gandhi, she does not like their coming to this house. She advises these two Muslim boys to go to Pakistan. Daksha has a habit of writing a diary, and she records her memory in her diary. The play probably opened in 1988, but through her diary, Mahesh Dattani presented the history and her early life in 1948. It is the diary through which the plot moves back to forty years ago. The play covers the life of Dakah from her youth to old. After knowing the real incident behind the fire of her friend's father's shop at the end of the play, she repents for it.

Smita Gandhi

Smita is the youngest member of the Gandhi family. She is the daughter of Aruna and Ramnik Gandhi. Smita is a college student, and she makes her friendship with Muslim boy and girl. Tasneem is her best friend, and Bobby, a Muslim boy, is also her friend. Her friendship with Muslim society is a shine of healthy relation between Hindus and Muslims communities at the time when both Hindus and Muslims kill each other. Both Javed and Bobby visit her. Smita is docile in the family as she behaves according to her mother's guidance, and outside the family, she is charming and energetic. At the end of the play, she charges her mother to enforce her rituals in her life.

Ramnik Gandhi

Ramnik Gandhi is the father of Smita and son of Daksha. He provides shelter and food to two Muslim boys, chased by the Hindu mob at the time of the riot. He is the owner of a saree shop in the market of Kapda Bazaar, and offers a job to Javed in his shop. When he realizes that Javed has thrown stones at the Rath Yatra, Ramnik wants to hand him over to the police or the Hindu mob. He knows the family's dark secret, and at the end of the play, he discloses it to his mother, Daksha. The secret is that the shop of Zarine's father was purposely set fire by his father, Hari, and his grandfather as they needed a shop for their saree business, and at present, Ramnik is the owner of this saree business. Thus the financial stability is based on the family of Zarine. This dark background of the family changed the character of Ramnik at the end of the play. He repents for the sin of his family.

Aruna

Aruna is the mother of Smita and the wife of Ramnik Gandhi. She is a religious woman and devotes her life to Lord Krishna. She is a traditional woman and wants her daughter, Smita, to follow her path of living. Aruna never likes Muslims in her life, and Javed and Bobby's presence in her house makes her uncomfortable. When she comes to know that her daughter, Smita, is a friend of Javed and Bobby, she asks her husband to stop the college of Smita. She pleads with Ramnik to ride away the Javed and Bobby from their house.

Javed and Bobby

Javed is the brother of Tasneem, and he is dropped out of school. He lives separately from his family as he is thrown out for his involvement in the riot. He was a smart boy, but a tragic incident has changed his life. Javed has been hired to attack the Rath Yatra. He is rude in behavior. Bobby is an educated Muslim boy who has just finished his college. Bobby is a friend of Smita and betrothed to Tasneem. Both Javed and Bobby come to Smita's house to meet her. At the end of the play, Bobby lifts the statue of Lord Krishna.

Zerine and Tasneem

Both Zarine and Tasneem are Muslim women in the play, *Final Solutions*. Both women never appear on the stage, and they are represented through the other characters of the play. Zarine is a close friend of Daksha. Her father is the owner of fruits and mithai shop. Like Daksha, she also loves music and a follower of Noor Jehan. Daksha visits her, and both friends gossip and sing-song together. Tasneem is a friend of Smita, and she is a college student. She lives in a girl's hostel. It is Tasneem who shares the life of her brother, Javed, with Smita. Tasneem is betrothed to Bobby, and both are going to marry. Both Zarine and Tasneem never appear on the stage, but their impacts are noticed in the play. It goes to the credit of Mahesh Dattani, who has created such back-stage powerful characters.

3

Bravely Fought the Queen

Bravely Fought the Queen is a popular play by Mahesh Dattani in the history of Indian theatre. It was first performed at the Sophia Bhava Hall, Mumbai, on 2nd August 1991. It is a stage play in three acts, and every act contains a title. Here Mahesh Dattani treats multidimensional areas of the Indian society. It is short but very important play as it deals with the contemporary issues. The play takes its setting from the urban society of Bangalore. The play is known for the treatment to modern capitalism.

Summary

Act I
The Women

The act I opens in a posh suburb of Bangalore in the house of Jiten Trivedi. A thumri song by Naina Devi is played and it is the background music. The house of Jiten Trivedi contains three bedrooms, two upstairs and one downstairs. Daksha, the daughter of Jiten, lives in the downstairs room, whereas one of the upstairs rooms is used by Dolly and Jiten, and another is by Baa, mother of Jiten Trivedi. Mahesh Dattani very craftily uses the stage to decorate the house of Jiten Trivedi. His brother Nitin Trivedi lives with his wife, Alka, in another house. This house has the same structure as the house of Jiten Trivedi. At the opening of the play, it is found that Dolly, wife of Jiten Trivedi, is getting ready for visiting to Kapoors, and she does her beauty mask on her face, and Baa, who is bedridden, sits in her room which is in upstairs of the house.

Dolly is visited by Lalitha. She is the wife of Sridhar, who is an employee of the advertising company ran by Jiten and Nitin Trivedi. Lalitha visits Dolly according to the guidance of her husband, Sridhar, and Jiten Trivedi. She is asked to discuss with Dolly about the masked ball. It is an important program for the Trivedi family as both Trivedi brothers will launch their new ReVaTee product. Both ladies are talking about the masked ball and the visiting of Kapoors. Dolly is talking about her visit of Kapoor's family and prepares for it, whereas Lalitha wants to discuss the masked ball. Dolly has experience with tailoring, and Lalitha wants to consult with her about the masks of the guests. Lalitha introduces herself with Dolly as the wife of Sridhar, who handles the ReVaTee account for her husband's business, and her bother-in-law, Nitin, calls him ReVaTee Sridhar because there are so many Sridhars in the office. The masked ball is the idea of Sridhar to launch the product ReVaTee. Lalitha defines ReVaTee as a new range of colour-coordinated nightwear and underwear for women. She also shares the story behind the origin of the name of ReVaTee. The name has been adopted from the name of the chairman's wife, Revathi, and when they were in Europe on holiday, the French couldn't pronounce her name correctly, and they used to call her Re-va-tee rather than Revathi. From this incident, the name ReVaTee has been originated. Lalitha shows Dolly the list of guests for the masked ball and most of them are known to her. Dolly knows the guests and has experience in tailoring; that is why her suggestion and contribution to the masked ball become essential for success.

Dolly informs about their aged family servant and his replacement by a handsome young boy, Kanhaiya, and her daughter, Daksha, who goes to school in Ooty. Their conversation is interrupted by the call of Baa from her room. Alka Trivedi comes to the house of Dolly. Alka is the sister of Dolly and sister-in-law of Jiten Trivedi. She marries Nitin Trivedi. After coming to her sister's house, Alka makes a phone call to the office to talk with her husband Nitin, and this call is received by Sridhar, who, after dropping his wife, Lalitha, at the house of Jiten, has gone to the office. When Dolly is dressing up to go, both Alka and Lalitha introduce themselves with each other, and she is shocked that all know the called off of their going to Kapoors, and Dolly is still dressing up. Dolly is a woman of short memory, and she easily forgets. Here she has forgotten postpone of their visit to Kapoors. Their going is called off, and Dolly has forgotten it, and she is dressing up. Through their conversation, Lalitha shares her hobbies with Alka. Lalitha is a writer of an occasional women's column for the *Times*, and her passion for the bonsai plantation. Alka is much smarter than her sister, Dolly, and she is addicted to alcohol and wine. She takes drinks and also serves to Lalitha. Alka rebukes Dolly for her docile character in the parties where Dolly sits in the corner to avoid the people. Lalitha gives a bonsai tree to Dolly as a presentation and guides how to care it. Dolly goes through the list of guests for the masked ball, and she considers the different masks for them. She thinks of the Shahs as astronauts, the Bedis as Laila-Majnu, the Mendens as Hansel and Gretel, Mr. Kashikar as Shivaji, and the Dutts as Raj Kapoor and Nargis. The three ladies involve in conversation, and it is interrupted by the repeated calls of Baa. Dolly and Alka talk about their brother Proful who has come in the city but he has not come to meet his sisters. Alka rebukes her brother, Praful, for spoiling her life. She reminds an incident of the rude conduct of her brother, Praful. Once Alka was dropped from school at home by a neighbour's son, and it was caught by Praful. He didn't say a word, but he lit the stove and pushed her face in front of it. Baa from her room cries out for Dolly. At the end of Act I, the three ladies are talking about the Daksha and Kanhaiya.

Act II

The Men

Act II opens in the office of Jiten and Nitin Trivedi. It is an advertising agency. Both brothers are discussing the launching of the ReVaTee, and its model Shirley. They are also talking about the visit of Lalitha to Dolly to discuss the ball as Dolly has some experience of tailoring, and most of the guests are known to her. Trivedi brothers are facing financial problems launching their ReVaTee in market, and they discuss over the arrangement of money. They think to take a loan from Nichani, but they can't afford the interest. But Jiten informs that their financial problem will be recovered by Praful, who is ready to provide money without any interest, and at the same time, they have no hasty to return the money. Praful is the brother of their wives, and he is also a close friend of Nitin. Here both brothers present a detailed description of the characters of Praful. They consider him as a sentimental fool. Praful is insulted by the Trivedi brothers, and he shows his generosity as he wants to help them. He is ready to give money at their crucial time. At the time of crisis, he comes ahead to rescue them. Here also, the crafty characters of the Trivedi brothers are expressed. They do not allow Praful to meet his sisters. He is informed that his sisters are out of the station, and they have gone to Ooty. Jiten makes a phone call to the hostel where Praful stays. He has come from Bombay, and Jiten settles a meeting with him tomorrow morning, and they will receive the money. Thus they attempt to solve their financial crisis. Then Sridhar enters the office. He has come after dropping his wife, Lalitha, at the house of Jiten to discuss the masked ball with Dolly, wife of Jiten.

Mahesh Dattani has used a complex technique to narrate the story of the play. The incidents of Act I and Act II are performed at the same time. After the arrival of Sridhar in the office, the phone rings and it is made from the house of Jiten Trivedi. Sridhar receives the call, and over the phone, Dolly is informed about the call off of their going. Here Dattani mixes the actions of the first act with the second act through the device of telephone. Dattani also makes complexity through the appearance of Baa and her chamber during the action of the play in this act. Dattani uses a complicated technique of theatre to present his action in the play. Sridhar is very serious about the success of the campaign, whereas its owners Jiten and Nitin, are not serious. Sridhar is very conscious of the negative reply of the board of directors, and he is planning to change the decision of the director board. Sridhar is also very serious with the market review regarding ReVaTee, and it is not affordable for women to buy a costly dress for sexual attraction to their men at night. But both brothers don't pay any attention to such negative reviews for their product. According to Jiten, their product will be purchased by men to present their women as the men have the capability to buy their products. Trivedi brothers stress on the subject of sexuality to launch their ReVaTee, but the board of directors considers it illogical, and the press calls it "offensive." While Sridhar gives importance to the market review and the Board of Directors' decision, Jiten denies such things, and Sridhar considers it as professional suicide. It is found that both Trivedi brothers have lack experience in the advertising business as they got in this business by chance. Somebody awed money from these brothers, and they took over his agency. Jiten suggests his brother Nitin to plead with their mother, Baa, to change her will to solve their financial crisis. In the will, Baa makes Daksha, her granddaughter as the official owner of her house, and on the other hand, both Jiten and Nitin want to sell the house to collect the money for their advertising ReVaTee. As Nitin is close to Baa, Jiten asks him to plead with their mother to change her will. Nitin shares a past accidental incident with Sridhar. Jiten is not a good driver, and once he was driving recklessly, the car toppled; an auto-rickshaw parked near the road, and the car hit a lamp post. Then the auto-driver grabbed Jiten, and in such a condition that the driver was killed in the accident. At the end of the second act, three men leave the office for the house of Jiten Trivedi.

Act III
Free for All!

This act opens in the house of Jiten Trivedi, and it contains the same setting as the first act. The change is noticed in the atmosphere outside the house, it is raining. Alka, after drinking alcohol, is lying on the sofa. On the other hand, Lalitha and Dolly talk about "Naina Devi" and "Jhansi ki Rani." Naina Devi was a thumri singer, and she belonged to the royal society. Naina Devi married in the royal society, and she lived a comfortable life and became a rajmata. But she had a fascination with the romantic song, song of love, and during this time, such songs were sung by whores and prostitutes. Generally, the royal family in India did not permit a royal lady to sing romantic songs, but for her extensive passion for music, Naina Devi was allowed to sing thumri and later became a renounced figure of a love song; she is called the 'Queen of Thumri'. The Jansi ki Rani is a historical figure in the history of India. She was a queen, but she led a masculine life, a life like a man. Rani Laxmibai was the queen of Jhansi, and she prevented the British authority to spread their colonial power in her territory. She knew the dignity of life and the importance of liberty. She sacrificed her life for her dignity, for her liberty, and for her state. Jhansi ki Rani Laxmibai fought against the British colonial authority and met a heroic end of life. Both Naina Devi and Jhansi ki Rani are the idol figures for Dolly and Alka. In the masked ball, Alka wants to dress like Jhansi ki Rani. She also wants to fight like a brave queen against society, her family, and her wretched condition of life. Alka asks her sister to make an armor of tin plate for her and a cardboard sword. Alka is fascinated with the rain, and outside the house, it is raining, and she goes out in the rain to enjoy it. She dances in the rain and becomes injured by leg. At that time, Jiten, Nitin, and Sridhar enter the house, and they notice her dance that makes a bad impression on the Trivedi brothers. Lalitha wants to leave the house, but it is raining heavily outside the house, it is not possible to go, and both Lalitha and Sridhar have to wait. Alka becomes bold in her conduct in the family, and she curses herself, her life, her brother, Praful, and the Trivedi brothers. She scolds her husband, Nitin, and her brother-in-law that her brother, Praful, is in the city and wants to see his sisters, Dolly and Alka, but Jiten and Nitin never allow him to meet his sisters. Jiten becomes irritated with the conduct of Alka. Here Mahesh Dattani makes his play very complicated as he stresses all the characters. All the characters perform together on the stage, and their conversations treat different topics. These may be categorized as the conversation between Baa and her son Nitin, the conversation between Jiten, Lalitha, and Sridhar, and the conversation between Dolly and Jiten. In the conversation between Dolly and Jiten, it becomes clear about the reason behind the deformity of Daksha. Dolly was beaten by Jiten at the time of her pregnancy, and Daksha was born two months premature with the cord around her neck. In the conversation between Baa and Nitin, two things become clear. The first is that according to his brother's suggestion, Nitin attempts to seduce his mother to change her will and requests her to will the house for him. In this regard, Nitin is ready to divorce his wife, Alka, to please his mother. The second important issue of this conversation is the secret of the identity of Dolly and Alka's father. It is Praful who hides the secret of their father at the time of the wedding. From a letter from her cousin from Ahmedabad, Baa is informed that their father is not dead. Their father lives with his first wife and four children, and Dolly and Alka's mother is his second wife. Dolly's mother is the whore of her father. Such background decreases the family reputation in society. In the conversation between Jiten, Lalitha, and Sridhar, the rude behavior of Jiten comes out once again. Lalitha is insulted by Jiten repeatedly, and Sridhar comes forward in defending his wife. The condition becomes very critical when both Jiten and Sridhar involve in a fight. Later Sridhar is suspended from the office by Jiten. Sridhar goes out of the house to arrange a car for their departure from the house of Jiten Trivedi. He rushes in the house as he witnesses an accident outside the house where a bagger is run over by a car. At the time of their departure, Lalitha clarifies the identity of cook boy, Kanhaiya, in the Trivaadi family, and it is clear that Kanhaiya is an imaginary character for Dolly. At the end of the play, Mahesh Dattani stresses on the relation between Nitin and Praful, and it becomes clear that both have a homosexual relation. Nitin has a deep fantasy about Praful rather than his wife, Alka. It also becomes clear that Praful, to hide their homosexual relation, married his sister, Alka, with his friend, Nitin.

Critical Analysis

Title

The phrase of the title possesses a masculine spirit. The term 'queen' stands for the feminine figure in the title, and the terms 'bravely' and 'fought' stand for the masculine quality. In this play, Mahesh Dattani refers to two masculine female figures from the history of India. The first one is Naina Devi. She was a rajmata or mother of the king, and belonged to the royal society where the passion for song especially for thumri was considered as a degraded art of life, and the women were prevented from listening and singing a love song. But for Naina Devi, the love song, especially thumri, stood for her art of passion, and she began to perform it and later established herself as a renounced figure and was called the 'Queen of Thumri.' Naina Devi was a bold figure, and she possessed a masculine spirit that helped her to go against the custom of the society, practiced thumri, and later identified with thumri. The second important figure is Jhansi ki Rani Laxmibai, an anti-colonial figure who fought against British colonial rule in the colonized India. She did not accept the British authority, and met a heroic death to save her dignity and sovereignty of life and her state. These two women figures are introduced here in this play to define the title of the play. In this play, Alka is a bold figure, and she possesses masculinity. Alka rebukes her mother-in-law, Baa for her pregnancy, and she charges Baa for not having any children. At the same time, Alka dances in the rain in society while her husband, her brother-in-law, and Sridhar come to the house of Jiten. In the masked ball, she wants to dress like Jhansi ki Rani, and it symbolizes her masculine spirit.

Domestic Relation

The *Bravely Fought the Queen* is a play based on the contemporary Indian society. It deals with the life of urban society and sets in a posh suburb of Bangalore. In this play, Mahesh Dattani shows the Indian traditional joint family system where complexity is common. In this play, Dattani identifies the complexity of the domestic relations between mother-in-law and daughter-in-law, between brother-in-law and sister-in-law, between husband and wife, and between brother and sister. Baa is a typical traditional mother-in-law who is known for her rude conduct with her daughters-in-law. She encourages her younger son, Nitin, to divorce his wife, Alka. According to the Hindu myth, the wife is the sole partner of the husband, but in the contemporary metropolitan society in India, the spiritual gap is a common matter. Such a spiritual gap between husband and wife is clearly explained by Mahesh Dattani through the relations between Dolly – Jiten and Alka-Nitin. The lack of intimacy between sister-in-law and brother-in-law is found between Dolly and Nitin and between Alka and Jiten throughout the play. The coolness between brother and sister after sister's marriage is noticed between Praful, Dolly, and Alka. The *Bravely Fought the Queen* is a domestic play that takes its setting from the urban society.

Structure

The play is divided into three acts, and every act has its own title. They are "The Women," "The Men", and "Free for All!". All the actions of the play take place in the house of Jiten Trivedi and in the office of Jiten Trivedi and Nitin Trivedi. It is an advertising agency. There are twin houses for the Trivedi brothers, but the play's action is performed in the house of Jiten Trivedi, and the house of Nitin Trivedi is mentioned in the play. The first act and third act are performed in the house of Jiten Trivedi, whereas the second act is performed in the office of an advertising agency possessed by the Trivedi brothers. The thumri music of Naina Devi is played in the play as the background music.

Backstage Characters

Mahesh Dattani is known for the creation of powerful backstage characters. These characters never appear physically on the stage, but their impact on the other stage characters is explicit. They behind the stage are controlling the main action of the play and motivate the actions of thc other characters. Here in this play, Praful is a backstage character whose impact is noticed on Baa, Trivedi brothers, Dolly, and Alka. Throughout the play, Baa is asking for Praful, and she eagers to meet him. Both Jiten and Nitin are also asking for financial assistance to launch their ReVaTee from Praful. They depend on Praful. Besides it, the marriage between Alka and Nitin is the result of Praful. It was Praful who enforced Nitin to marry his sister Alka. Another backstage character of this play is Daksha. She is the deformed daughter of Jiten and Dolly. She never comes on the stage, but her impact is noticed in the play. Both Trivedi brothers need money, and they have decided to sell the house of Baa. But the house is given to Daksha by Baa. Thus she dominates her father and uncle.

A Post-modern Play

The *Bravely Fought the Queen* is a postmodern play that deals with contemporary capitalist society. The postmodern society is known for hyper-reality and simulation. It is a trend in the postmodern society to present reality in such way that it seems to be more real than the reality. The advertising companies, through the advertisements, represent their products in a more realistic way to create a market to sell the products. The reality becomes hyper-real, and it is very difficult for postmodern people to find out the reality. French cultural critic, Jean Baudrillard (1929-2007) identifies such a gap between reality and presentation, and he calls it 'simulacra.' In this play, *Bravely Fought the Queen*, Mahesh Dattani very artistically highlights this topic. Both Trivedi brothers will launch their underwear product, ReVaTee, for women, and in this regard, they need to advertise to create a market for their upcoming product. So both Jiten and Nitin hire Shirley as their model to launch their product. In the postmodern capitalist society, the Board of Directors and market reviews or customer reviews play significant roles behind the success of any product in the market. Here Mahesh Dattani stresses these two issues for the success of ReVaTee. The Trivedi brothers have received a negative reply from the Board of Directors and negative customer reviews from the market. Yet, they are ready to launch their product ReVaTee which is considered financial suicide by the experts like Sridhar. The masked ball, advertising agency, model Shirley, Board of Director, and market review stand for the postmodern capitalist and urban society. It is noticed that in the postmodern Indian society, frankness about sexuality, especially in the advertising agencies, is a common matter. The advertising of sexual products like a condom is displayed publicly. Such frankness is also found in the play, *Bravely Fought the Queen*, where Jiten Trivedi hires a beautiful model, Shirley, to catch the customers' attention. Besides this, the ReVaTee will be used by women for the sexual attraction to their men. Women will buy it to satisfy their husbands' sexual urge, or men will buy it to present their wives as a sexual gift. The postmodern society is a society of futurism where the violence, speed, and splendor of war are celebrated. Futurism is an Avant-Garde movement, originated in Italy to celebrate violence based on modern technology. In this play, the futuristic element is found through the rash driving of Jiten, who hit his car with the post and killed an auto-rickshaw driver. At the end of the play, Sridhar notices that a beggar is run over by a car. In the postmodern society, road accidents are the common matter, and reckless driving is a futuristic concept that celebrates speed in society.

Women's Empowerment

Mahesh Dattani is known for the feminist touch in his plays. He very craftily explains the lives of women throughout his plays. In this play, *Bravely Fought the Queen*, he portrays the life of domestic women. Dattani explains the rift between husband and wife and how a wife is dominated by husband. Both Dolly and Alka are neglected by their husbands, Jiten and Nitin Trivedi. Dolly has been brutally beaten by her husband during her pregnancy and gave birth to their deformed daughter, Daksha. Nitin hates his wife, Alka, and he is ready to divorce her. Both Dolly and Alka are unknown about their husbands' business. Such relations show the complicated domestic life where the wife is dominated by the husband. The life of the woman in the house of her in-law also becomes complicated for the mother-in-law. Such a situation is narrated by Mahesh Dattani through the relation between Baa and her two daughters-in-law, Dolly and Alka. Baa asks her younger son, Nitin, to leave his wife, Alka. In short, in this play, Mahesh Dattani describes the life of domestic women.

Queer Element

The next important issue in the play, *Bravely Fought the Queen*, is to deal with the subject of gay. Praful and Nitin have intimacy, and such a relation in Indian society is considered a queer relation. To hide this immoral relation from society, Praful played a trick with his friend, Nitin, and younger sister, Alka. He has given married Nitin to Alka so that Praful can hide his homosexuality in society. It is another reason behind the weak relation between Nitin and Alka.

Escapism

Escapism and isolated life are the common features of postmodern society. In this play, Dolly wants to escape from reality through the music of thumri by Naina Devi. She has a fantasy about the imaginary young cook boy, Kanhaiya. Dolly's personal satisfaction in life is the music of thumri and Kanhaiya. Alka is also dissatisfied with her life, and she also wants to escape from the reality of life. Throughout the play, Alka is in her drunken mood and takes wine. She is intoxicated and attacks the customs of the family. She criticizes her husband, her brother, and mother-in-law. It is the wine through which Alka escapes from the harsh reality of her life. The *Bravely Fought the Queen* is about postmodern capitalism and its impact on domestic relations. In contemporary society, women are exploited by their men for financial benefit in business. Women are forced to make relations in the capitalist society by their men with clients and bosses in the urban capitalist society in India. Such an example is presented in this play by Mahesh Dattani. For the ownership of Baa's house, Nitin is ready to leave his wife, Alka, because this ownership provides him and his brother, Jiten, sufficient money to overcome their financial crisis to launch their women's product, ReVaTee.

Characters

Baa

Baa is the oldest character in this play. She is a widow and the mother of Jiten Trivedi and Nitin Trivedi. Baa is bedridden, and throughout the play, she is in her room. Baa lives with her sons, and at present, she is with her elder son, Jiten Trivedi, and will live with her younger son, Nitin, in his house. Baa is a typical mother-in-law, who does not like her daughters-in-law, Dolly and Alka. She is also not too much passionate with her sons. Baa has willed her house to Daksha, her granddaughter. Neither Jiten nor Nitin is the successor of her property. The conjugal life of Baa was not satisfactory. She was beaten by her husband. Mahesh Dattani has used a typical technique to represent Baa in his play. She never comes to the main portion of the stage, but she frequently appears throughout the play. The stage light falls on her chamber, and she makes frequent conversations with Dolly, Alka, Nitin, and Lalitha. Baa financially dominates her sons, who need money to launch their product, ReVaTee, and it is Nitin who attempts to seduce her so that she may change her will and give the house to him. In this regard, Nitin is ready to leave his wife, Alka, to please his mother as Baa does not like Alka. Throughout the play, Baa is asking for Praful, whom she entrusts more than her sons.

Dolly

Dolly is the wife of Jiten Trivedi and the mother of Daksha. At the beginning of the play, she is preparing for a visit of Kapoor's family. Dolly is a woman of low memory and has forgotten that the visit is called off. She is a docile woman, while her sister, Alka, is bold. At the parties, Dolly avoids the meetings with people and sits corner in the party. Her relation with her husband, Jiten, is not charming, and she has to face her husband's brutality. She was beaten during her pregnancy by her husband, Jiten. Dolly has some experience with tailoring, and Lalitha visits her to discuss the masked ball. Her suggestion is much important for the Trivedi brothers for the success of the masked ball. Dolly is a music lover, and she loves the thumri song, and her favourite singer is Naina Devi. She has a fantasy for the young cook boy, Kanhaiya, but this cook boy is an imaginary character of Dolly in this play.

Alka

Alka is the sister of Dolly and Praful, and younger daughter-in-law of Baa. She is the wife of Nitin Trivedi. Alka is much smarter than her sister, Dolly, and she is bold in her conduct. Alka loves wine and drinks ram, and throughout the play, she is in the intoxicated mood. She has no child, and is a dancer who likes to dance in the rain. It is Alka who complaints against her in-law's family. She does not like her brother, Praful, and rebukes him for spoiling her life. Alka also rebukes Baa for not having a child as Baa does not allow her son, Nitin, to have so. Alka once was beaten by her brother, Praful, during her unmarried life when she was caught coming to college with the neighbour boy. In the masked ball, she pretends to dress like Jhansi ki Rani, and it symbolizes her revolutionary character. Alka rebukes her husband and brother-in-law, Jiten, for hiding the secret of Praful's arrival to the city and not allowing him to meet them.

Lalitha

Lalitha is the wife of Sridhar, and she pays a visit to Dolly according to the suggestion of her husband, Sridhar, and Jiten Trivedi to discuss the masked ball. She is a good wife, and assists her husband in his office work. Lalitha has a passion for the bonsai plantation and writes articles for the women's column in *Times*. She presents a bonsai tree to Dolly, and instructs how to take care of the bonsai tree. Lalitha is standing against Dolly and Alka, who are unknown about the office works of their husbands, whereas Lalitha knows everything about Sridhar and his office. In this play, Lalitha is insulted by Jiten, and it is Sridhar who comes forward to defend the dignity of his wife whereas both Dolly and Alka are repeatedly insulted by their husbands, Jiten and Nitin Trivedi.

Jiten Trivedi

He is the elder son of the Trivedi family. Jiten is rude in conduct and crafty in nature. He has no experience in the advertising business, and he, with his brother, Nitin, will launch a women's product, ReVaTee. To solve the financial crisis, he will take a loan from Praful, and at the same time, Jiten is not allowing Praful to meet his sisters. Besides it, Jiten suggests his brother, Nitin, seduce their mother, Baa, to change her will. He wishes to manage the money by selling the house of Baa. During the pregnancy of his wife, Dolly, Jiten has beaten her, and it causes the deformity of their daughter, Daksha. As a businessman, Jiten stresses sexuality to launch the product, ReVaTee. He denies the importance of the board of directors' decision and negative market reviews for their product. His rush and hasty decision to launch the ReVaTee may be the cause of failure.

Nitin Trivedi

Nitin Trivedi is the brother of Jiten Trivedi, and he is the husband of Alka. Nitin is directed according to his brother, Jiten, and his mother, Baa. His relation with his wife, Alka, is not satisfactory. According to the suggestion of his brother Jiten, Nitin is talking with his mother to change her will, and on the other hand, to please his mother, he is ready to leave his wife.

Sridhar

Sridhar works in the office of Jiten and Nitin Trivedi. He is the husband of Lalitha, whom he drops at the beginning of the play at the house of Jiten Trivedi to discuss the masked ball with Dolly, wife of Jiten Trivedi. He has deep marketing knowledge and knows the importance of the Board of Director's opinion and market reviews for launching a new product in the market. He works under the Trivedi brothers, but he has deep experience in the advertising business than his masters. For launching the ReVaTee in the market, Sridhar attempts hard for comfortable circumstances for its success, but his masters don't show any interest in his seriousness. Sridhar as a husband is much better than Jiten and Nitin. He shares his issues with his wife, Lalitha, and she also assists him. Both Sridhar and Lalitha are saving money for their new house. While Lalitha is repeatedly insulted by Jiten, he comes forward to defend the dignity of his wife and fights with Jiten. Later Sridhar leaves the job. In short, Mahesh Dattan uses Sridhar as an opposite character from Jiten and Nitin Trivedi.

Praful

Praful is the powerful figure in the play, *Bravely Fought the Queen*. He plays his role behind the stage and dominates the main action of the play and the characters. Praful is the brother of Dolly and Alka, and he hides their family secret from all the characters. The secret is that their mother is the second wife of their father, who lives with his first wife and has four children. When Baa knows this secret, she makes the lives of her daughters-in-law very critical. As a brother, Praful does not like that his sisters make friendship with a neighbor boy. When the Trivedi brothers face financial problems to launch their product, ReVaTee, Praful comes forward to assist Jiten and Nitin. He is ready to loan them money. In the play, Praful is not liked by Jiten, and Nitin is his close friend. Both Nitin and Praful have a fantasy for each other, and to hide this fantasy in society, Praful has married his sister, Alka, to Nitin. For Baa, Praful is the most trusted person rather than her sons. Throughout the play, Baa is asking for Praful, and she wants to meet him because she considers Praful the right person who can look after her granddaughter, Daska, and her house. In short, Praful is the most dominating character in the play.

4

Tara

Tara is a play about gender discrimination in a family where the son is given priority rather than the daughter. It was first performed at the Chowdiah Memorial Hall, Bangalore, under the title, *Twinkle Tara*, on the twenty-third October 1990. The Playpen Performing Art Group was the troop to perform this play. In this play, Mahesh Dattani stresses the position of the daughter in the family and sharply criticizes the ideology that prefers son rather than daughter in the family. Thc plot deals with lives of a twin, Tara and Chandan, Tara's tragic death, and Chandan's life as a writer. Chandan is a biographer of his twin sister, Tara.

Summary

Act I

For the theatrical presentation, Mahesh Dattani has used a multi-level set. The stage is divided into different parts, and every part contains some significant action throughout the play. The lowest level occupics a major portion of the stage that represents the house of the Patels. It is the family which is used by Mahesh Dattani as the background for the play. Here Dattani very craftily utilizes the time for the presentation. The house of Patels and the actions related to this house are presented through the memory of older Chandan. The next level of the stage belongs to s suburb London where bedsitter Chandan who has changed his name from Chandan to Dan, sits and reminds his past life and his dead sister, Tara. In this regard, Mahesh Dattani makes the action very complicated to understand the action. The suburb of London is the only realistic level in this play, and through this level, the actions of other levels are presented. The major action is performed in the house of Patels, but it is the Dan (Older Chandan) in London through which the actions in the Patels' house are presented to the audience. In short, the play is a psychological journey of Chandan where older Chandan in London retreats to his adulthood and describes the tragic incidents of his own family. On the high level of the stage, there is a chair in which Dr Thakkar remains seated throughout the play, but he is unconscious about the play's action. He remains on the stage, but he doesn't watch the actions of the play. The other portion of the stage belongs to the street outside Patel's house.

The play opens in a suburban area of London where Dan (here, Dan refers to the older Chandan in London) is busy with his biographical writing about his sister, Tara, and he entitled it as the *Twinkle Tara*. He is a writer, and here Mahesh Dattani provides some information about the ideology of Dan regarding his theory of poetry and drama. Dan reads loud his work, *Twinkle Tara*, a drama in two acts by Chandan Patel; copyright, Chandan Patel, 93 Fishpond's Road, Tooting, London SW177LJ. Then the play's action moves from London to India, and it opens in the house of Patels in Bombay. It is presented through the memory of Dan, who retreats to his past life in India where he with his twin sister, Tara, shifts to a new house in Bombay, and they have to unpack their luggages. In Patel's house, both twins, Tara and Chandan are playing a game of cards, and in this game, Tara wins, and Chandan charges his sister, Tara, for cheating in the game and for his defeat. Bharati, their mother has finished her morning pooja or prayer, and Patel, their father is checking his office bag and starts for his office. The new house yet to be decorated properly as the family just sifted their new house. Tara is physically weak, and she is under the treatment of Dr Kapoor, and her mother, Bharati, is very conscious about the health of Tara, and she enforces her daughter, Tara, to take milk, but Patel is bothered for such conduct of Bharati for their daughter, Tara, who seems to be fine and healthy as the doctors are satisfied with the progress of Chandan and Tara. The progress of Tara and her twin brother, Chandan, is mentioned in a medical journal by doctor Kapoor, and their progress is a rare incident in the history of medical science. Both Tara and Chandan have just finished their tenth exam and are waiting for the results. Patel asks his son, Chandan, to come office to assist him in office work, and he denies the priority of Tara in the office. But Chandan suggests to his father that Tara is the best option for him to assist in office rather than him because Tara possesses a business quality mind and whereas Chandan is not so much intelligent as Tara. Here Tara becomes very critical with the system that the male members of the family are responsible for earning whereas the females stay home to look after children and cooking from the ancient time. Their conversation is interrupted at the arrival of a neighbour girl, Roopa.

Roopa, Premala, and Nalini are the neighbour girls of Tara and Chandan. Here Mahesh Dattani shows the influence of Hollywood movies on the young generation. Young people like Roopa, Chandan are fascinated with Hollywood movies, and Roopa visits the house of Patels to watch movies like *Snow White and the Seven Dwarfs* and *Fatal Attraction*. Roopa has attachment for the Hollywood movies, and Bharati offers her to watch movies in her house if Roopa becomes a good friend with her daughter, Tara, and comes continuously. Roopa likes to watch horror movies where monsters like oglers play essential roles. Oglers are monsters with one big eye in the middle of their foreheads. Roopa comes to know about Chandan's habit of writing about the biography of his twin sister, Tara. Patel is very serious about his children's health and is bored with blinded caring of his wife, Bharati, of his children, especially Tara, who is weaker than Chandan.

Then the play's action moves from the memory of Chandan to older Dan in suburb London, from Bombay India to London. Here Chandan clarifies the injustices done for Tara both by his family and by nature. Mahesh Dattani, through Chandan here, introduces another important character of the play Dr Umakant Takkar. Dr Thakkar and his medical team performed the surgery to separate Siamese twins, Tara and Chandan. Dr Umakant Thakkar is a renounced child specialist, and he is known for his outstanding work at the Queen Victoria Memorial Hospital in Bombay. He has also been associated with the many major hospitals in the USA, most notably the Children's Hospital in Philadelphia. He visits India, and during his stay at the Queen Victoria Hospital, he was the surgeon-in-chief of the most unique and complex surgery, the first of its kind in India. It was that surgery where Tara and Chandan were separated from each other as they were born as Siamese twins or conjoined twins. Such a kind of twin is rare in the history of medical science. Here Dattain presents a medical definition of Siamese twin through Dr Thakkar. Here Dattani makes an interview between Dr Thakkar and Chandan as a reporter on the subject of the Siamese twin. After the surgery, both Tara and Chandan possess two artificial legs each, and for her artificial leg, Tara has to face criticism in society by the neighbour girls, Prema, Nalini, and Roopa.

The action moves to the memory of Chandan' Patel and his house in Bombay. Here both Tara and Chandan are talking about their surgery in Bombay when they were babies. The Patel family has come to Bombay two times. For the first time, they had come for the surgery to separate Tara and Chandan, and they now have come for the second time for the kidney transplant of Tara. Roopa makes a visit to Patel's house, and here Mahesh Dattani provides information about the family background of Patel. Roopa has finished her ninth, whereas Chandan and Tara completed tenth and are waiting for the results. They belong to Bangalore, and now they have come to Bombay. The marriage between Patel and Bharati is an inter-caste marriage, and for this marriage, there is a rift between Patel and his family. Bharati is from Bangalore, and Patel is a Gujarati, and he left his parents because of this marriage. The father of Bharati was an influenced person, and he was an industrialist and an MLA. At present, Patel is the general manager of Indo-Swede Pharmacia, the biggest pharmaceutical company in the country. This is the background of Patel's family. Tara informs Roopa that she is going to surgery on her kidney, and a transplant will be made soon. In their conversation, Roopa asks Tara to make distance from the other neighbour girls, Prema and Nalini, who mock her artificial leg that was exported from Jaipur. It is Bharati who seduces Roopa to have a friendship with her daughter, Tara. She offers Roopa to come and watch movies with Tara, but Roopa is the best friend of Prema and Nalini. She later criticizes Patel's family in the presence of Prema and Nalini. There would be a kidney transplant for Tara in Bombay, and Patel makes arrangements for a donor, but Bharati pretends to donate her own kidney to Tara. Patel prevents his wife from performing such an act, but Bharati is blind to donate her kidney.

Here the abnormal condition of Bharati is clearly expressed, and she feels very worried about hiding a secret from their children. Both Patel and Bharati hide a family secret to Tara and Chandan, and Bharati wants to disclose it to them, Patel prevents her from doing so. This secret relates to the surgery by which both Tara and Chandan were separated. The play's action moves on Tara, Chandan, and Roopa, and all three are watching a Hollywood movie, *The Mirror Cracked*. Here Mahesh Dattani refers to the poem the "Lady of Shallot" by Alfred Lord Tennyson. They are gossiping on the subject of daughters in the community of Patel, where the daughters are killed by feeding excessive milk so that they can show the reason that the daughters are died for eating milk. Here Bharati is very conscious about the career Tara. In the meantime, Patel comes home from the office and rebukes Bharati for not controlling Tara and Chandan, who are spoiling time by watching movies. Patel strictly guides Chandan to come office to assist him in work, whereas Chandan shows his interest in not going to the office without Tara. Patel also plans for Chandan for his higher education in abroad. Chandan will go to London for his education, where uncle Praful will help him to gate admission to a university and to settle his career. Patel never plans anything for Tara and for her career. Bharati plans everything for Tara, and she never allows Patel to plan for their daughter. Patel rebukes Bharati for her blind love for Tara that spoils the life of Tara. The play's first act concludes with the debate between Patel and Bharati on the subject of a career of Tara and Chandan; and Bharati's blind love for Tara.

Act II

For Act II, Mahesh Dattani uses the same stage setting and both acts contain the same stage decoration. It begins with a passionate conversation between Bharati and Tara. Bharati loves her daughter very much, and she is going to donate her kidney to Tara. After this brief conversation between mother and daughter, the play moves to older Chandan (Dan) and Dr Thakkar. Here Dr Thakkar explains his successful surgery to separate Patel's twin. Dr Thakkar provides a detailed explanation of medical complexity to separate Tara from Chandan. Then the play moves to Patel's house, and Tara returns home after her kidney transplant. Bharati is absent in the house, and Tara asks for her mother, who is admitted to the hospital. Here Mahesh Dattani uses a complicated technique to represent the play. Dattani stresses several issues at a time. The play narrates the house of Patel, Tara's return from the hospital after her kidney transplant, a conversation between Roopa and Prema in the street about the family of Patel, and Dr Thakkar's description of the medical condition of Patel's Siamese twin. Both Chandan and Patel attempt to hide the incident that has happened with her mother, Bharati, who is now admitted to the hospital. In the absence of Bharati, Patel cares for his weak daughter, Tara, and at least Tara is ready to act according to her father, Patel, but she also wants to stay with her mother in the hospital. Patel makes arrangements for physiotherapy for Tara and Chandan. Patel makes a plan for his Chandan in England, where he will be sent under the guidance of Praful, who will manage to get admission and to get a scholarship in England. Both Tara and Chandan have inherited a legacy from their grandfather in Bangalore. The scene of the play focuses on a conversation between Tara and Chandan. Chandan does not want to go to college without Tara as he scares to meet new people. They also call neighbour girls Roopa, Prema, and Nalini as oglers, who criticise their artificial legs from Jaipur. Tara misses her mother and begins to cry.

The next important scene of the play is found between Chandan and Roopa. Both are gossiping on the subject of

Hollywood movies like *Fatal Attraction* and *Sophie's Choice*. They are also talking about the importance of gender in the family. Roopa is asking about Tara and Bharati's return from the hospital. During their conversation, Chandan attempts to seduce her. He touches the breast of Roopa that frightens her, and she begins to rebuke Chandan. In the meantime, Tara returns home, and Roopa informs Tara about the sexual harassment performed by her brother, Chandan. She charges Chandan as a rapist. Later both Tara and Roopa involve in a quarrel, and Roopa informs that she comes to the house because she has been asked to come by their mother, Bharati. Tara shows her interest in being a social worker and wants to join Mother Teresa. She is ready to sacrifice her life for those thousands of poor sick people on the roads. Tara says to Chandan that she has visited the hospital to meet her mother, Bharati, but the hospital staffs have not allowed her to meet with Bharati. Patel has strictly guided the staffs not to allow Tara to meet his wife, Bharati. Tara rebukes Chandan for not visiting their mother in the hospital. She also asks Chandan to help her to visit their mother at the hospital. Patel has come home from the office during their conversation, and he is asking for their physiotherapy, and he comes to know that both Tara and Chandan have not gone for physiotherapy. He also knows that Tara has visited to the hospital to meet Bharati that shocks him. Then Patel shares the past incidents about the family, his marriage with Bharati, his father-in-law, and the birth of Tara and Chandan as twins. He also gives a detailed description of the surgery. The twins were born with three legs, and a scan showed that a major part of the blood supply to the third leg was provided by the girl. For the reconfirmation, another report was done, but the result was the same; the third leg belonged to the girl rather than the boy. Bharati and her father did a private meeting with Dr Thakkar about the surgery, and in this meeting, they decided to take a risk to give two legs to the boy rather than the girl, and the doctor gave his approval for the surgery. The result was that Chandan had two legs for two days and one leg for Tara. It is Bharati for whom Tara has one leg, and she has lost her another leg. Later Patel came to know that the intention of the doctor behind this wrong surgery. The doctor had acquired three acres of prime land in the city's heart to start a large nursing home in Bangalore. It was the grandfather of Tara who used his political power to get a land for the doctor in the city. With the reveal of the family secret, the play concludes.

Critical Appreciation

Tara is a play that deals with versatile themes. Generally, it is a play about gender discrimination in the family and society, but it shows the corruption in the medical system in India; and the play deals with the theme of repentance. The title of the play is based on the central character, Tara. She is the deformed daughter of Patel's family. The title is appropriate and the plot describes the life of its central character. The play covers the life of Tara from her birth to her death. Here Dattani highlights the misjudgements against Tara by the society as well by her family. Her twin brother, Chandan, also wrote a biography of Tara in the play entitled *Twinkle Tara*. In this play, Mahesh Dattani very craftily criticizes the corruption in the Indian medical system where for personal benefit, the doctors perform wrong surgery. Dr Thakkar knows very well that the extra leg medically fits to Tara, and to give Chandan it means a big mistake in the surgery. As he plans for the largest nursing home in Bangalore, Dr Thakkar accepts the proposal of Bharati and her minister's father. He is well familiar with the result of the surgery, yet he for his nursing home does the surgery. Such action shows the big mistake in the medical system in India where the life of the patients is used for the financial and career benefits for the corrupted doctors like Umakant Thakkar.

It is a play about the patriarchal society where the males are given priority rather than the females. In an ideal society, both males and females should have equal priority, but the females are pushed towards a subservient position for the society where the families like Patel are living. In such a society, the girls are killed by feeding excessive milk. It is a silent murder that the girls have died of overeating. At the time of surgery, a choice has come for Bharati. As twins, both Tara and Chandan possess the third leg, and after the scan, it becomes clear that this extra leg belongs to Tara. The Patel family prefers Chandan rather than Tara, and this extra leg was given to Chandan at the time of surgery, though this leg didn't fit Chandan medically. Here Bharati choices a deformed daughter rather than a deformed son. Here Mahesh Dattani criticizes such philosophy in the Indian domestic life where girls are neglected by their parents. Tara is the symbol of all the neglected daughters in India.

The next important subject of the play is repentance. This theme is expressed through the character of Bharati. Once, she performed an injustice against her daughter, Tara. At the time of surgery, Tara has lost her leg and became a deformed girl for her mother, Bharati. If Bharati didn't force Dr Thakkar to give the third leg to Chandan and if it was given to Tara, perhaps Tara would possess two legs. Bharati's wrong decision makes her life unrest, and at the time of the second surgery of kidney transplant, Bharati wants to give her kidney to Tara though there is a donor of kidney for Tara. After the surgery of the twin, Bharati repents for her wrong decision against Tara. The theme of repentance is also found in Chandan. Older Chandan repents for the immature death of his twin sister, Tara. He knows it very well that his mother, Bharati, betrayed Tara at the time of their surgery because of him. For him, Bharati took the leg from Tara, and it was Chandan who worked unknowingly behind the deformity of Tara.

Characters

Tara

Tara is the titled figure of the play. She is the deformed daughter of Patel's family and the twin sister of Chandan. Tara is an intelligent girl who is the winner of the game of cards. Chandan considers her as the perfect businesswoman. In school, Tara helped her brother to manage for a peaceful student life. Tara loves her mother, Bharati, who is responsible for her deformity. Her relation with the neighbouring girls, Roopa, Prema, and Nalini, is not harmonious. Tara is criticized for her artificial leg by the neighbour girls, and she quarrels with Roopa, who charges her brother, Chandan, as a rapist. After the successful kidney transplant, Tara wants to join Mother Teresa for social work. It becomes her dream to work for the people on the road. At the time of her first surgery, where she has been separated from her twin brother Chandan, Tara was betrayed by her own mother, Bharati, her minister grandfather, and Dr Thakkar. She is a neglected daughter of Patel's family. At first, she is neglected by her mother than her father, Patel. For her career, Patel doesn't plan anything, whereas he makes plans for Chandan. Patel wants Chandan to join the office, and he will go to England for her higher education. But for Tara, he does nothing.

Chandan/Dan

Chandan is the twin brother of Tara. In this play, aged Chandan is called Dan. He is an author and writes a biography of his sister, Tara. Mahesh Dattani presents the main plot of the play through the memory of older Chandan. He is also deformed like his sister, Tara, and possesses an extra artificial leg from Jaipur. In the game of cards, he is defeated at the hand of his sister, Tara, who he considers a businesswoman. After completing his education in India, he migrated to England for a higher study, where he settled and established himself as a writer. He has written the biography of his sister, Tara, under the title, *Twinkle Tara*. In India, young Chandan denies going to college without Tara because he faces problems of meeting new people in college, and it is Tara who helps him recover from this problem. Young Chandan attempts to seduce Roopa, a neighbour girl in Bombay who later charges him as a rapist.

Bharati

Bharati is a passionate mother of Tara. She is the wife of Patel and daughter of an industrialist and minister. She is a domestic woman and takes extra care of her daughter, Tara. At the time of Patel's twin's surgery, Tara has lost her leg and became deformed permanently for her wrong decision. Later she repents for this incident; at the time of the kidney transplant of Tara, Bharati eagers to donate her kidney to Tara. As a mother, Bharati never allows her husband to make plans for Tara and her career. She looks after everything for the life of Tara. Bharati seduces Roopa to come to their house and make friendship with her children, Tara and Chandan. Bharati faces a deep mantel pressure and is hospitalized, where Tara is not allowed to visit her mother.

Patel

Patel is the father of Tara and Chandan. He is a Gujarati, and for his marriage with Bharati, he has separated from his family and lives with his wife, Bharati, son, Chandan, and daughter, Tara. He is working as the general manager of Indo-Swede Pharmacia, the biggest pharmaceutical company in the country. He asks Chandan to come office until his school opens again. Patel plans for his son, Chandan, and his career in England, but he does not plan anything for his daughter, Tara. He rebukes his wife, Bharati, for spoiling children's lives as she is unable to look after them properly. Patel is unable to challenge the decision of his wife, Bharati, in the matter of Tara and Chandan. At the time of the surgery of their twin children, he didn't dare to challenge his wife's decision to give the third leg to Chandan, which medically fitted for Tara. Besides it, he knows that Bharati's extra care may spoil the life of Tara, and he never opposes this care. For Tara, Patel doesn't plan anything regarding her future.

Dr. Umakant Thakkar

He is an excellent child specialist and possesses a prestigious reputation in India. He has been associated with major hospitals in the USA, most notably the Children's Hospital in Philadelphia. He belongs to the team of doctors who performed the surgery to separate Tara from her twin brother, Chandan. He is a reputed but corrupted doctor. For his dream to have the largest nursing home in Bangalore, Dr Thakkar supported the wrong decision of Bharati at the time of surgery.

Roopa, Prema, and Nalini

They are the neighbour girls of Patel's family. Among these three girls, Roopa regularly visits the house of Patel, and she has a fantasy about Hollywood movies, movies of monsters, especially oglers. Roopa is asked to be a friend of Tara and Chandan by Bharati. She and the other two neighbour girls are shocked to know that Tara and Chandan have artificial legs. Roopa is seduced by Chandan. All three girls quarrel with Tara.

5

Dance Like a Man

Dance Like a Man is a very beautiful play based on the theme of dance and its different meanings in India after the liberation from British colonial rule. Here Mahesh Daatani shows the different views of dance through the three generations of the Parekh family. It is a play about two acts, and here Mahesh Dattani very craftily mixes past and present incidents. He uses a shawl and newspapers as the indicating marks between past and present. The play, *Dance Like a Man*, was first performed at Chowdiah Memorial Hall, Bangalore, on 22nd September 1989. It was a part of the Deccan Herald Theatre Festival. The play was accepted very heartily by its audience.

Summary

Act I

The play opens in an old-fashioned house in the heart of the city. It is possessed by Jairaj Parekh. This family is known for its nationalist background as his father, Amritlal Parekh, was a liberalist and social reformist who fought against the British colonial rule in India. It is a family of renounced traditional dancers. Jairaj, his wife, Ratna, and his daughter, Lata, are all traditional dancers. The play opens in the present time, and Jairaj lives with his wife, Ratna, and daughter, Lata, in this old-fashioned house. In the opening scene, Viswas comes to the house of his fiancée, Lata Parekh. He intends to meet his future parents-in-law to discuss their relation, but both Jairaj and Ratna are not present at that moment, and they have gone out. Both Lata and Viswas are discussing their future marital life. Viswas is the son of a sweet maker, and his father runs a mithai shop (sweet shop) on the commercial street, and his father is a quite successful businessman. But it doesn't matter for Lata and her family because Viswas will be selected if he allows Lata to dance after their marriage. Both Ratna and Jairaj are very conscious about the career of Lata as a dancer rather than the legacy or property of her future husband, Viswas. At the same time, Lata informs Viswas that Lata is the sole heir of this old house, and at the present, this old house is very much precious. A Marwari builder offers Jairaj for ninety lakh for this house, and the builder wants to build a shopping complex, but Jairaj has denied this offer. For Jairaj, this house possesses memories of his past life and his father. It is a heritage to him from his father. It contains a lot of memory of Jairaj. Lata shows the hallroom of this house where Lata's parents practiced under the guidance of their guru, and she also shares how she was enchanted with the dance moves of her parents in her childhood while she watched them to dance. Through their conversation, Lata makes very clear to Viswas about the children in their marital life. She assures Viswas that they will not have children very early after their marriage. They will wait for it until the proper settlement of Lata's career as a dancer. She also informs Viswas that she was born when her parents were forty years old. Here Mahesh Dattani has pointed out the psychology of the urban society where the career is given priority rather than the domestic life. In this society, the relation among the family members is very weak as they give priority to their career and artificial life rather than the harmony of the domestic life. Mahesh Dattani also focuses on the inter-caste marriage system in contemporary India. The upcoming marriage between Lata and Viswas is an inter-caste marriage. Lata Parekh is a Gujarati, whereas Viswas is Southie (South India). Lata informs Viswas about her grandfather, Amritlal Parekh. Her grandfather was a freedom fighter and social reformist, and he was a possessive person who always dominated his son, Jairaj. This house witnessed political secret meetings during the British Raj in India. Armitlal Parekh led these meetings. Lata also says Viswas that her father, Jairaj, has deep affection and respect for his father, and for this reason, he will not sell this house. Most of the furniture of this house belongs to the time of Amritlal Parekh, and the house is an antique in the city. In short, Lata provides all the information of her family's traditional and socio-political backgrounds to her future husband, Viswas.

Lata makes a phone call to her Muthu uncle to inquire about her parents, Jairaj and Ranta, who are absent in the house, and Viswas has been expected to visit them as he has an appointment with her parents. She comes to know about the tragic incident over the phone that one of their musician, C. V. Srinivas, a mridangist, has broken his arm. This incident is a big problem for the Parekh family as Lata will perform a public show, and this show will never be completed without a mridangist. Viswas notices the cupboard where old books and a shawl are preserved, and Viswas is attracted to the shawl. He asks Lata it as a dowry, but Lata assures him that he will never be given the shawl by her parents. The shawl contains a prestigious memory and reputation for the Parekh family. For Mahesh Dattani, this shawl plays the most important role in changing the setting of the play. With the help of it, Dattani has shifted the story from present to past, from old Jairaj to young Jairaj. Lata says about the history of a shawl. It was presented to Amritlal Parekh from the Mysore maharajah. Her grandfather got this and an award from the maharajah at the time of Dussehra. While Lata is in the kitchen, the phone rings, and Viswas receives the phone call. It is the call from Chaganlal Chadani, who is a builder and wants to buy the Parekh's house, but Viswas assures him that Jairaj still has not changed his mind to sell the house. After a short conversation between Viswas and Chaganlal Chadani over the phone, Viswas takes the shawl from the cupboard. He wears it and begins to act like father, Amritlal Parekh, and son, Jairaj Parekh. Here Viswas imitates Amritlal and Jairaj through his act and speaks on dance like a father and a son. In the meanwhile, Jairaj and Ratna enter the house, and they watch the acting of Viswas, who becomes embraced for his abnormal manner in the house of Parekh. He puts off the shawl, and Ratna takes it from him and puts it in the cupboard. Both Jairaj and Ratna are talking about a problem that may destroy their long-run plan for their daughter, Lata. They are organizing a great dance program to launch their daughter, Lata, as an eminent figure in the Indian classical dance, and only ten days are remaining for the preparation. In the meantime, their musician C.V. Srinivas, their mridangist, has broken his arm. This program may be performed without a flutist or violinist, but it is impossible without a mridangist. If they can't manage a mridangist for Lata's performance, they may have to postpone their program, and Lata will never receive a great start for her career as a dancer. At least both Ratna and Jairaj decide to hire Seshadri for the performance of Lata from Chandra Kala. They are also talking about the close relation between Chandra Kala and Seshadri, which has been caught by Jairaj when they were in Moscow on a dancing tour. All these conversations are listened by Viswas, and he seems to be a bit worried and puzzled at their conversation, and he breaks his silence. Ratna is under deep mental pressure, feels a headache, and to recover from it, she takes Aspro. Jairaj asks her not to take too much Aspro. He also advises her not to worry about Lata's performance. But Ratna is very serious about the performance and debut of Lata as a dancer. They have only ten days for the preparation, but their mridangist will not perform. In the performance, they have invited the President of India as chief guest, and it becomes impossible for Ratna to inform him that the function has been postponed. Mahesh Dattani very artistically explains the psychology of contemporary parents who are very serious about their children's careers. At the present time, most of the parents are in trauma about the future of their next generations. For this trouble for Lata's function, Ratna considers her father-in-law, Amritlal Parekh, and his curse. Amritlal never determined dance as a perfect option for a career, and he never allowed his only son, Jairaj, to have a career in dance. It is his curse that is responsible for the problem of Lata's career. Here Ratna asks her husband to be a man, and she still considers him as a boy. In the mid of their conversation, Viswas wants to go, but he is stopped by Jairaj, and takes out a bottle of whiskey from the cupboard, and both Jairaj and Viswas begin to drink. Jairaj asks Viswas about his life and future, and in a reply, Viswas informs him that he has not yet started his life. He is the son of a Mithaiwalla, and his father saved enough money for his future from their traditional business. Jairiaj also shares with Viswas how his father Amritlal saved money and increased his property through buying houses and bungalows when the British colonial authority left India at the dawn of Indian liberation from the clutches of British colonialism. Viswas asks Jairaj for the dowry of the shawl, but Jairaj assures him that he will take it at the time of their marriage, not now. Viswas leaves the house of Parekh.

Lata is in fast sleep, and Ratna finds out drunkard Jairaj, and later she also assists in drinking with her husband. Here both Ratna and Jairaj talk about their past lives and their struggles to establish themselves as dancers. Jairaj reminds Lata of her uncle, who attempted to seduce Ratna when they lived for a short period in his house after leaving the house of Amritlal Parekh. Jairaj attempts to remind Ratna about Shankar, but it irritates Ratna, and she changed the topic of their conversation. She prefers of talking about the performance of Lata and wishes to talk with Chandra Kala for Seshadri. She is worried about the future for her daughter, Lata. As they have no enough time for the debut of Lata and there is no chance to recover their mridangist C.V. Srinivas.

Here Mahesh Dattani has changed the play's setting, and the story moves from present to past, from old Jairaj and Ratna to young Jairaj and Ratna. Here Dattani changed the time, but the setting of the play is the house of Amritlal Parekh. Mahesh Dattani uses the shawl for the flesh back story in the family of Parekh. Wearing the shawl, old Jairaj becomes Amritlal Parekh, and Viswas becomes young Jairaj. Thus the shawl helps Mahesh Dattani to change the setting of his characters. Here young Jairaj is practicing his dance under the guidance of his guru in the house of his father, Amritlal Parekh. Both Jairaj and his wife, Ratna, practice dance in the presence of musicians. On the other hand, Amritlal Parekh is a traditional man. He is an activist and fought against the British colonial rule in India. He is also a reformist and works for the reformation of women, especially temple women or devadasi. In the higher class society, dance is regarded as the art of prostitutes and lower rank people. Jairaj belongs to the elite Hindu society, and his passion for dance decreases the reputation of Parekh's family. The dance guru of Jairaj and other musicians in the house irritate Amritlal, who is regularly visited by the special guests, including politicians who consider the dance as an art of lower class. Amritlal wants to stop it and asks Jairaj to ride away his guruji as soon as possible as he is expecting some elite people in his house. The rift is noticed between father and son for dance. Jairaj transforms the library hall into a dancing hall where he rehearsals for his decent performance, and he also grows his hair to perform a dance form, Kuchipudi, and in this dance form the men dress up as women. Amritlal asks his son to be a man and wants to make a cricket pitch, but his son likes to dance and transforms the house into a gathering place for dancers and prostitutes. Amritlal Parekh is a freedom fighter and fought for the liberty of India, but in the family, he grabs the liberty of his son, Jairaj. He dominates Jairaj and attempts to stop his dance. Amritlal considers that there is no future for dance, and his son, Jairaj, is spoiling his life and time on dance. At the same time, for his passion for dance, the reputation of the Parekh family is gradually decreasing. Amritlal asks his son if he is dancing under the influence of his wife, Ratna. In the traditional point of view, the dance belongs to the art of prostitute and temple dancers. They are known for their sexuality and also belong to the backward class in society. As a reformist, Amritlal Parekh works for this class and reforms the society for them. He builds ashrams for them where they are educated and provided food and shelter. But Jairaj has an adverse view for dance from his father. The dance for the temple dancers and devadasi stands as the main life-stream for them, and if they are put in the ashrams and are not allowed to dance, then the society will lose its tradition. The dancers should be allowed to dance and as well as be awarded for their art. Jairaj says that his father, under the name of reformation and education in the ashram, is destroying India's culture. He also asks his father to return the home and art to the temple dancers. The next important conversation is between Ratna and Amritlal. Ratna informs that according to the suggestion of guruji, Jairaj grows his hair to perform the dance from Kuchipudi and the long hair of Jairaj embraces Amritlal, who wants to shave the head of his son. Ratna every Monday goes to the temple of Lord Shiva, but she visits to the house of Chenni Amma instead of to the temple to practice the dance. It has been caught by Patel, who later informs about it to Amritlal, who does not like the visiting his daughter-in-law to Chenni Amma and her practice in her house as the people can look at her dance. It is a disgraceful act that a woman from elite society dances publicly. For Ratna, Chenni Amma is an excellent dancer, and she is now seventy-five years old. She is the oldest living exponent of the Mysore school and doesn't have a single student who is dedicated enough to absorb her knowledge. She is old enough, and nobody visits her. Chenni Amma spends her time at the temple steps and sells flowers, and when she comes to know that Ratna is a dancer, she pleads with her to learn the art of abhinaya from her. This is the main reason that Ratna every Monday goes to the house of Chenni Amma instead of to the temple. Amritlal becomes irritated with the passion of his son and daughter-in-law, and he is worried about the future of his generation. He repeatedly asks them to ride away the musician from the house. It becomes clear to Jairaj that for his father, he will never be a successful dancer. At least he with his wife, Ratna, leaves his father's house for a fresh atmosphere where he and his wife can practice their dance and lead the life of dancers. The last episode in the play concludes with the departure of Jairaj and Ratna from the house of Amritlal Parekh. At the end of the act, Mahesh Dattani changes the setting of his play. The stage returns to the present. It moves from young Jairaj to old Jairaj. Both old Jairaj and Ratna are preparing for sleep, and Ratna is talking about the lending of Seshadri from Chandra Kala. Thus the act one concludes.

Act II

The setting for Act II is the same as Act I. In the house of Amritlal Parekh both acts are performed. Act II begins in the past rather than the present. There are found changes in the characters of Amritlal and Jairaj. In Act I, Jairaj leaves the house of his father with his wife, Ratna, and Act II begins with the return of Jairaj and Ratna to the house of Amritlal. But this time, Jairaj is defeated and proves incapability to provide food and shelter to his wife. He fails to secure the life of his wife. Some changes are also noticed in Amritlal. He gives permission to practice dance in his house and allows to practice in the library hall. Amritlal also gives permission to visit his house to guruji twice a week in the morning. Here Mahesh Dattani shows the marriage based on the theme of compromise of career and it is noticed in the character of Ratna. It is the earnest will of young Ratna to be a successful professional dancer. This becomes clear in the conversation between Amritlal and Ratna. She has married Jairaj because she is allowed to dance and Jairaj is also himself a dancer. Thus it is the dance for that Ratna has married to Jairaj. Dattani also shows the selfish nature of the character of Ratna. While Amritlal asks her to help him to make Jairaj a man and stop his career as a dancer, he also assures Ratna that he will never stop her from dancing; then, Ratna also assures that she will assist Amritlal to make Jairaj as a man. This is one kind of agreement where both Amritlal and Ratna have signature. Amritlal does so because he wants to make Jairaj a man, and Ratna does it for her career as a dancer.

The time in this play once again changed, and this time Mahesh Dattani uses the newspaper to move from past to present. Amritlal picks up the newspaper, and he becomes old Jairaj on the stage. Thus the setting of the play moves from past to present. For the present situation in Act I, Dattani narrates the preparation of a dance program organized by Ratna and Jairaj to debut their daughter, Lata, as a classical dancer, and in Act II, Mahesh Dattani continues it, and here he narrates the story after the performance of Lata. The gap between these two acts is ten days. In Act I, Dattani explains Ratna and Jairaj ten days before the performance and their problem to manage a mridangist, whereas, in Act II, Dattani narrates the situation after the successful performance of Lata. Dattani shows that the performance is done before starting the act two, and Lata has been successfully debuted as a dancer. Lata becomes a star of classical dance overnight. The newspapers and articles buzz with Lata's performance, and she has received good critical reviews from the critics of dance. The President of India gave a standing ovation to Lata for her excellent performance. Dr Devaraj Gowda, a famous dance critic, has already given a good compliment to Lata. He is busy with his organization of the Indian festival in Canada. He also informs that Chandra Kala is one of the selection committee members, and her daughter, Mala, has already been selected for this festival. Another famous critic of dance, C.V. Suri, also passed a good review for Lata's performance. Both Jairaj and Ratna are talking about the success of their daughter's performance, the good critical reviews in the statements like *Herald*, *Times*, and *Express*.

Lata wakes up from her sleep, and she is applauded by her parents. Ratna talks over the phone to Seshadri, who played mridang during the performance of Lata, and he asks for an apology for playing the wrong tala during Lata's performance. Then Viswas comes to the house of Parekh, and he is very excited about the success of Lata and good reviews from the dance critics. Lata wakes up from a deep sleep after her great performance, and she is greeted by Jairaj, Ratna, and Viswas. Lata shares her experience with them as a dancer on the stage, and it becomes clear that she is not a talented dancer as she has forgotten her last dance step or jathi and simply posed till the music finished during her performance. It shows that Lata is not an excellent dancer and her parents are the main reason behind her success. Later they are talking about the erotic formation of dance, and such formation has been noticed by Viswas during the performance of Lata. Here Jairaj shares his experience as a female dancer as he performed a dance in the female costume in an army's camp. Ratna becomes emotional with the success of her daughter, Lata, and she begins to cry. Here Ratna has been criticized by Jairaj for her behavior after the success of Lata. She cuts the papers that contain the reviews of Lata's performance and wants to paste them to the family album. But Jairaj urges Ratna to have a personal album for Lata to paste her own memories as she deserves it. Jairaj also attacks Ratna for their dead son, Shankar, but Ratna feels irritated at the reference of Shankar.

Mahesh Dattani moves the action from present to past, from old Jairaj to young Jairaj. At this time, young Ratna is a popular and successful dancer, and she is highly demanded for programs. On the other hand, Jairaj failed as a dancer, and he is waiting for his wife in the house and takes drinks. Here one thing is clear that Ratna has succeeded in her mission to assist Amritlal to break the dream of her husband, and in return, she has been assisted by Amritlal to become a successful dance. She is busy with her performances, and both Jairaj and Ratna have a son, Shankar. Shankar is looked after by an ayah as Ratna has no time for her son. Every night the cry of Shankar is stopped by the ayah with the help of opium that is harmful to the baby, and in the contemporary elite society where the children are looked after the ayahs, it is common to use opium to stop the cry of the children at the time of their sleep. For the excessive use of opium by the ayah Shankar has met a premature death. Here Ratna, for her career as a dancer, sacrifices the life of her son, Shankar. In the drunken mood, Jairaj criticizes Ratna for spoiling his career as a dancer. He mocks his wife for her assistance to his father, Amritlal, to make him a man and destroy his passion for dance. Jairaj says that it is Ratna who forced him to perform in his weak techniques. At the same time, Jairaj says he has been neglected on the stage shows while he performed with his wife. Here it becomes clear that Jairaj is a passionate dancer, whereas Ratna is an ambitious dancer. It also becomes clear how high ambition dominates the passion of dance through the relation between Jairaj and Ratna. Act II and the play end at the present time with old Jairaj and old Ratna, and the Parekh family is ready to move to their new flat.

Critical Appreciation

Title

The title of any work is most important as it is a mirror to represent the subject matter. Here Mahesh Dattani has used an appropriate and perfect title for this play. The phrase of the title is "Dance Like a Man." In the Hindu mythical and cultural society, the subject of dance has different meanings. According to Hindu mythology, Lord Shiva is known as the god of dance, and lord Shiva's mythical dance form is Tandav. In mythology, the dance thus receives a masculine background. Lord Shiva is one of the Hindu tridaves, and he is known for his destroying power. But for the Hindu cultural society, the subject of dance is considered as a feminine art. It belongs to the prostitute society, and it is considered as an art for the erotic culture. The dance belongs to the culture of devadasi and temple dancers. For this feminine and erotic background in Hindu cultural society, the dance is recognized as an art that destroys the family's reputation. Throughout the play, Mahesh Dattani very craftily focuses on the theme that a woman easily succeeds in the world of men, but for a man, it is not easy to establish himself in the world of women. Jairaj has a passion for dance, and it is his dream to recognize himself as a reputed classical dancer. As in the Indian Hindu society, the dance is regarded as a feminine art; it becomes critical for him to establish himself as a dancer. He is attempting his career in the world of women, and it is not easy for him to be a successful dancer. He performed the dance as a woman, wearing the costumes of Ratna during his performance in an army camp. Jairaj dances like a woman rather than a man. He grows his hair to perform the Kuchipudi dance. It is a feminine dance form. For dance, Jairaj becomes a woman, and in this play, Mahesh Dattani asks to dance like Lord Shiva and to imitate his dance form, tandav. The title indicates that a man should dance like a man, not a woman. As the dance is a feminine art, it is easy for Ratna to succeed and popularize as a classical dancer. In this play, Mahesh Dattani shows how the ideology of dance has been changed according to the change of time after India's liberation. It is a play about the three generations of the Parekh family. Amritlal Parekh belongs to the first generation. He is a traditionalist and freedom fighter. For him the dance belongs to lower-ranked people, and it is an erotic art for prostitutes. His consideration for the dance is negative and believes that the reputation of his family decreases for his son, who wants to be a dancer. Jairaj belongs to the second generation, and for him, dance is a passion. He finds his life incomplete without dance. For dance, he leaves his house, and when he fails to be a successful dancer, he begins to take drinks to forget his agony. Lata belongs to the third generation of the Parekh family, and for her, dance stands for the profession rather than passion like her father, Jairaj. Throughout the play, Ratna and Jairaj are struggling to establish her as a successful professional dancer. A great program is organized by Ratna and Jairaj to debut her as a dancer. Mahesh Dattani presents different notions of dance according to the change of time.

Passion and Treachery

In the play, *Dance Like a Man*, Mahesh Dattani explains the themes like passion for dance, a career as a dancer, and treachery. Here Dattani very skilfully explains these themes. Jairaj is a character through whom Dattani explains the spirit of passion and for dance he is ready to sacrifice anything. He is a dancer and also helps his wife to be a dancer. But for Ratna, dance is not a passionate art; she is a compromised dancer. For her career as a dancer, she compromises with Jairaj; she has married Jairaj because he is a dancer, and he allows her to dance. Ratna also compromises for the second time with Amritlal for her career as a dancer. Amritlal is a traditional man and never accepts his son as a dancer, and he asks Ratna to assist him in making Jairaj a man. In this regard, Ratna assists Amritlal as he allows her to dance. Here Ratna for her career compromises with Amritlal, and she also betrays with her husband. Jairaj as a husband gives importance to his wife's interest for dance, allows her to dance, and assists Ratna as a dancer; but on the other hand, when the time comes for Ratna's assistance to her husband, she cheats with her husband. Jairaj never thinks of his wife, Ratna, as an unsuccessful dancer, but for her own career, Ratna destroys the passion of Jairaj and is responsible for the unsuccessfulness of Jairaj as a dancer. In this play, Mahesh Dattani very craftily explains how Jairaj's passion is destroyed by his treacherous wife, Ratna. In Hindu philosophy, a wife is considered the half soul of her husband, but the relation between Ratna and Jairaj is different. Ratna is not the half soul of Jairaj.

Children and Metropolitan Society and Children

Mahesh Dattani is very critical for the parents and their role towards their children in the urban society. In this society, the children are neglected for the passion of career by their parents. The children are not properly treated by their parents as they are busy with careers and business. In this play, Mahesh Dattani has very beautifully pointed out the outworn relationship among the family members in the urban society through the family background of Amritlal Parekh. In this society, the children are given priority after the career of the parents. The children are looked after by the ayahs rather than their parents. Jairaj and Ratna are the parents of Shankar and Lata. Ratna was a successful popular dancer when Shankar was a child. His mother was busy with her programs, and child Shankar was looked after by his drunken father, Jairaj, grandfather, Amritlal, and an ayah. It was the ayah who gave opium to stop the cry of Shankar every night. As a result, Shankar met his early death. Here Mahesh Dattani shows that for her career as a dancer, Ratna was unable to manage time to look after her son, Shankar. In the urban society, it is a belief that for the children and domestic duties, parents are not able to achieve their goals. The domestic disharmony has been lost that is very technically explained by Dattani through the Parekh family for the career-oriented life. Besides it, Lata is going to marry Viswas, she also clarifies about children to Viswas after their marriage. Lata assures Viswas that they will have children after the establishment of hcr career as a dancer. Thus for both Ratna and Lata, the children are hindrances to their careers as dancers.

In the urban society, the children are planned children. The parents are very conscious when they should take children. A couple plans everything about the conjugal life before the marriage. Here Lata and Viswas do so before their marriage. In such a society, the children are forced to act according to the wishes of their parents. The children have no liberty to lead a life according to their choice, and on the other hand, the parents plan everything about their children when and what to do. Lata is the only daughter of Jairaj and Ratna. She is debuted in this play as a dancer and begins her career as a dancer. But it is her parents who have worked behind her success. Lata is a planned daughter in the Parekh family. It is her parents who worked behind her success as a dancer. Ratna is tensed about her daughter's career, and here she is the representative of all the parents in the contemporary metropolitan society who are very conscious about their children's careers.

Characters

Amritlal Parekh

Amritlal Parekh is the head of the Parekh family. He belongs to the elite Hindu society. Amritlal is a freedom fighter, liberal, and social reformist. He has held meetings in his house with activists and leaders. In this play, Amritlal is the representative to the Hindu traditional and patriarchal society. He is the father of Jairaj. The relation between father and son is controversial as Jairaj is a dancer. Dance is a feminine art, and Amritlal wants to make his son a man, and he asks his daughter-in-law, Ratna, to assist him in making Jairaj a man. Amritlal fought for the country's liberty against the British colonial rule, but in the family, he grabs his son's liberty. As a social reformist, Amritlal works to reform the temple dancers; he builds ashrams for them where they are given education.

Jairaj Parekh

Jairaj Parekh is a passionate dancer, and he is the only son of Amritlal Parekh. For his passion for dance, his relation with his father is not satisfactory. He is a son who revolts against his father. Against the will of his father, Amritlal Parekh, he continues his dance. He leaves his father's house when Amritlal asks him to ride away his guru and the other musicians from the house. He is a defeated husband for Ratna. He was unable to provide food, shelter, and security after his departure from the house of Amritlal with his wife, Ratna. He has a passion for dance, but he is an unsuccessful dancer. He dances like a woman rather than a man. Jairaj grows his hair to perform the feminine dance from, Kuchipudi. He also dances in the female costume for the army. Jairaj has inherited a huge property, including the Parekh house, from his father. He denies the offer of a Marwari to sell the house. Jairaj possesses an antique shawl gift, and he wants to give this shawl to his future son-in-law, Viswas. He criticizes Ratna for the death of their son, Shankar, and spoiling his career as a dancer. He also criticizes Ratna after the successful performance for Lata when Ratna wants to paste the paper's cuttings in the family album.

Ratna Parekh

Ratna Parekh is the wife of Jairaj and mother of Lata. She is also a dancer. She has married Jairaj to start her career as a dancer. Later she makes an agreement with Amritlal Parekh for establishing her career as a dancer. It is she who assists Amritlal to destroy the passion of Jairaj as a dancer. Ratna is an irresponsible mother for Shankar and a responsible mother for Lata. For her negligence as a mother for Shankar, Parekh's family has lost their son, Shankar. The death of Shankar makes her life unrest, and she avoids the subject of Shankar when Jairaj wants to talk about it. As a responsible mother, Ratna is very conscious of the debut of Lata as a dancer. She arranges a grand program for Lata.

Lata Parekh

She is the daughter of Jairaj and Ratna. Lata is betrothed to Viswas, a son of a sweet maker. Lata is the future star of classical dance. Her parents arrange a grand dancing program to debut her as a classical dancer. Her performance has got good reviews from the dance critics, and she has also received a standing ovation from the President of India. Before the marriage, she makes clear to Viswas about their children. She, with her future husband, Viswas, plans her conjugal life.

Viewas

Viswas is the son of a Mithaiwala or sweet maker. He is going to marry Lata Parekh. He does not care about dance, but Viswas is the future son-in-law to Parekh's family, a family of classical dancers. After the successful debut of Lata as a dancer, he is excited too much. Viswas asks for the dowry of the antique shawl from Jairaj, and he will receive it at his wedding to Lata.

Bibliography

Agrawal, Beena. *Mahesh Dattani's Plays: A New Horizen in Indian Theater.* Jaipur: Book Enclave, 2008. Print.

Agrawal, Dipti. *The Plays of Mahesh Dattani: A Study in Thematic Diversity and Dramatic Technique.* New Delhi: Discovery Publishing House Pvt. Ltd., 2013. Print.

Chaudhuri, Asha Kuthari. *Contemporary Indian Writers in English: Mahesh Dattani.* New Delhi: Cambridge University Press India Pvt. Ltd., 2008. Print.

Das, Bijay Kumar. *Form and Meaning in Mahesh Dattani's Plays.* New Delhi: Atlantic Publishers & Distributors Pvt. Ltd., 2012. Print.

Dattani, *Mahesh-Collected Plays,* Vol. I & II, Penguin Books, New Delhi: 2000.

Dhar, Subir. "Where There's a Willand Bravely Fought the Queen: The Drama of Mahesh Dattani" in *The Plays of Mahesh Dattani A Critical Response(eds.)* R.K. Dhawan & Tanu Pant. New Delhi: Prestige Books, 2005.

Kuthari, Choudhuri, Asha. *Plays of Mahesh Dattani Contemporary Indian Writers in English Mahesh Dattani.* New Delhi: Foundation Books Pvt. Ltd., Cambridge House, 2005.

McRae, John. "A Note on the Play" *Collected Plays Mahesh Dattani.* New Delhi: Penguin Books, 2000.

VIJAY TENDULKAR

1

Kamala

Kalama is a play of two acts on the subject of inhuman women's auction in contemporary society in India. Vijay Tendulkar is a socialist playwright, and he is identified with the title 'Social Commentator'. Here Tendulkar stresses on the life of subaltern people. It is a play about the domination of the tribal society by the civil society. The play shows the silent role of the authority and government on the system for the inhuman women's market in modern India.

Summary

Act I

The *Kamala* is a play on the silent role of government on the subject of women's auction. It takes its setting in the capital city of Delhi. It opens in the morning in a small bungalow in the fashionable city of New Delhi. It is Neeti Bagh in New Delhi where Jaisingh Jadhav resides with his wife, Sarita, and all the action is taken in the drawing-room of this residence. Kamalabai is the housemaid of Jaisingh. But some actions are performed behind the stage and they are informed, for example the Press Conference in the Press Club is informed rather than it is acted on the stage. Jaisingh is a journalist, and he is out of Delhi to collect some information for sensational news. He works as an Associate Editor in the English language daily. Kakasaheb, Sarita's uncle, has come to Delhi for some business, and he stays at the residence of his niece, Sarita. He is a sixtyish gentleman. He is also a journalist. He was born in an aristocratic family, but he lived a simple life under the inspiration of

Mahatma Gandhi. The play opens in the morning, and Kakasaeheb receives calls and informs that the owner of the residence, Jaisingh is out of Delhi. Sarita enters the drawing-room with breakfast for Kakasaheb. Both are talking about the subject to note down the phone calls. The phone rings again, and this time, Sarita receives the call. She comes to know about the Press Conference at the Press Club. Sarita receives one after another call and writes down all calls in her notebook. It is not easy for her to remember all calls, and it is a common factor that a residence of a journalist receives many calls, so she notes during the absence of her husband. While her husband comes home, Sarita hands over the recorded notebook. Sarita receives a call from the office of Jaisingh, and it is Surinder from the office who informs Sarita that Jaisingh left Ujjain last night and he may come at any moment. She calls out for their maid, Kamalabai, and instructs her to prepare the birth room and cooking for the master of the house, Jaisingh. It is a problem for Sarita that she needs servants from her home town, Phaltan. She can't feel comfortable with the local servants. Her mother wishes to have servants from her native town that provides her mother confirmation about her daughter's safety. Besides it, she has some problems speaking Hindi and Punjabi. So she asks a servant from her native town. Both Kakasaheb and Sarita are talking about journalism. Kakasaheb is also a journalist, and he considers himself a dead journalist. He talks about the changes which are noticed in present-day journalism. He is an aged journalist and can find out the modifications in journalism from past to present. For Kakasaheb the present-day journalism is high-speed journalism, and it is suitable for young people like Jaisingh. It is a time for the running fast, to overcome one by another. Here Kakasaheb attempts to find out the faults of contemporary Journalism. In the absence of Sarita, the phone rings and this time, Kakasaheb receives the call. It is a threatening call for Jaisingh, and the caller hides his identity. This threatening call has come for the news against an M.P. from Madhya Pradesh on the twenty-third, which was published by Jaisingh. He wrote the article for the M.P. who suspected his servant of theft and locked him up, and gave him a thrashing. Here

Kakasaheb asks Sarita to be conscious about the security of life. He also suggests Sarita hide identity in the paper so that readers can't understand the reporter's identity and people can't threat for such news. It is unnecessary to show the news under the real name of journalist He may use the phrase "From Our Correspondent". But Sarita informs Kakasaheb that Jasingh is a bold journalist and prefers to write under his name. It is Jaisingh determination to write everything under his name, and if the editors would forget to print his name, then Jaisingh nearly would resign from his job. Sarita also informs that these threatening calls are common from them. It becomes habitual for her to receive such calls. Kakasahed asks Sarita to have an arm or gun with Jaisingh or to inform the police. But Sarita replies that Jaisingh has no gun, and it is useless to inform the police because half of them involved in these threatening calls. Sometimes Sarita becomes upset about these calls, but Jaisingh does not bother about these calls.

Jaisingh returns home with a village woman. She is Kamala, the titled character of the play, and she belongs to the tribal community and is an Adivasi woman. Kamala wears a dirty white sari, and her face is under a veil. She carries a bundle in the crook of her arm. Kamala sits in the corner of the drawing-room. Jaisingh is tired and travel-stained. He shares his journey, missing the night train, chasing it in a private taxi, and catching it at Donpur. Jaisingh notices Kakasaheb and inquires when he has come and shows his greetings to Kakasaheb, who informs him that he has come the previous day and would leave the next day. Jaisinngh asks Sarita about the phone calls during his absence in the house and is handed over the notebook of the phone calls by Sarita. Kakasaheb informs Jaisingh about the threatening phone call for his twenty-third paper, and Jaisingh takes it very casually. He makes a call to Jaspalji and shares the success of his journey. He is on some mission, and it seems to be completed that becomes clear from the phone call of Jaisingh to Jaspalji. Here he talks about the sensational news, the Press Conference, Kamala as the centre of this conference, and the preparation of his team for this Press Conference over the phone. After the call, Jaisingh involves a conversation with Kakasaheb, who asks him to be conscious about the threatening phone calls. Kakasaheb informs the reasons for his visit to Delhi, and he has come to get a quota of paper for his magazine. Jaisingh wants to help Kakasahed to get the paper's quota as the Secretary of the Department is his friend, and he will make a call to do it quickly. Both Kakasaheb and Jaisingh are talking about the risky life of the journalists. Kakasaheb repeatedly asks Jaisingh to be conscious about the security of life. Jaisingh reminds Kakasaheb about the ideal life of Journalism as he is a journalist, and during his youth, Kakasaheb fought against many battles against British rule and went to prison for his support to the Indian revolution. During these days, Kakasaehb did not have any body-gourd for his safety. Here Kakasaheb has pointed out the enemies of a journalist. In the old days, the enemies were open, and they could be identified. But today, the situation has been changed, and the enemies can't be identified as they hide their identities. They hide in the darkness, and the present time is a difficult time for journalists. The attention of the people in the room falls on Kamala who is eating. Jaisingh asks Kamala if she needs more food or tea. Kakasaheb wants to know about thc identity of Kamala from Jaisingh, who avoids Kakasaheb and does not share the actual identity of Kamala. Jaisingh goes for birth, and Kakasaheb and Sarita also exist from the room except for Kamala. The phone rings and Kamalabai rushes into the drawing-room to receive the call, but it is disconnected. Kamalabai asks Kamala about her identity, her residence, and intention of coming there. Kamalabai comes to know that she is Kamala, and she has come from the village Karimsharif near Luhardaga. Kamalabai becomes shocked when she realises that Kamala has been bought there by Jaisingh from a bazaar. After completing his bath, Jaisingh enters the drawing-room and informs Sarita that Kamala may stay with them for that day. He asks Kamala about his residence, and Kamala likes it very much, and she considers it as a palace. It is a royal place for her, and she likes to stay there and wants to do some little work. Kamala is a village woman, and she is an innocent. Jaisingh shares his secret mission with his wife, Sarita, and informs her that he has bought her for two hundred and fifty rupees from the Luhardaga bazaar in Bihar, where the subaltern Adivasi women are sold like cattle in the open market. The men who want to buy, they at first inspect them. All kinds of women are sold in such markets. When Jaisingh was in this market, Kamala had no customer, and he has bought her from this market for two hundred fifty rupees. Sarita is shocked, and Jaisingh assures her that many people like her do not know this market and this dark system in civilised Indian society. The police know it's true, but they don't want to admit it. They mock the reporters that for the sensation news, they create such rumour in the society. The government is also silent about it. Jaisingh and his team know it, and to make clear evidence in the society, Jaisingh went there to collect evidence against the human tracking, and he has bought Kamala as a proof to prove it. This Kamala will be presented as a witness in the Press Conference. Jaisingh first wrote about it, but he did not have any definite facts; the police washed their hand, and the Home Minister puts his hands over his ears. Here Jaisingh proves himself as a bold journalist and criticises the roles of the police and the government. The Press Conference is very important for Jaisingh, and after the conference, the situation will be normal again. The conversation between Jaisingh and Sarita is interrupted at the ring of the doorbell. Jain, a fellow journalist of Jaisingh, visits and asks about the trip. Both Jain and Jaisingh are talking about their profession of journalism. But Jaisingh hides his secret mission for the Press Conference and Kamala to Jain, who leaves the residence of Jaisingh after a short time and assures that they will meet at the Press Conference. After the departure of Jain, Jaisingh asks about Kamala, and Sarita informs him that she is in the room of Kamalabai and wants to give some hot water for her birth. But Jaisingh stops her and suggests that Kamala will take her bath after the Press Conference in the night or the next day. He wants to present Kamala with her dirty clothes in the evening Press Conference to highlight the reality of the tribal life and women's auction.

Here Vijay Tendulkar brings some modifications to the stage. The stage becomes dark, and the time is afternoon. The action moves from morning to afternoon. The scene of the play is still the drawing-room of Jaisingh's residence. Kaksahed is in on the sofa, and Jaisingh seems to be strolling about, lost in thought. Jaisingh is ready for the Press Conference and asks Sarita for Kamala, but Kamala is sleeping. She comes to the drawing-room after the repeated calls of her master, and she is very obedient to her master. Jaisingh asks her to be ready for out, and Kamala shows her eagerness to go for either Krishna temple or Rama temple. But when she comes to know about the Press Conference and she is the central figure of this conference she denies to go. She likes to go tomorrow. Jaisingh makes her ready for the conference and guides her how to deal the Press Conference. At the conference, she will sit on the chair, people will clap for her, and she will be asked questions about her village, domestic life, food, clothes, and daily life. At least Kamala becomes ready for the Press Conference, and she asks for a sari to Sarita as she is wearing a rag one. But Jaisingh asks her not to change her dress and urges her to attend the conference in the same clothes she is wearing now. Jaisingh plans to present tribal life and its problems in the Press Conference and to have the reality of his information; he wants to present Kamala with her rage clothes to catch the people's attention at the Press Club. Both Jaisingh and Kakasaheb are talking about the motif of journalism, and they share different views on the ideology of journalism. They talk about the role of journalism for the reformation of society as it points out the dark sides of society. Journalism brings both danger and profit for its people. It also provides financial stability in family. For example, Jaisingh lived in the shed outside a house in Karol Bagh five years ago, and now he is living in a bungalow in Neeti Bagh. Journalism not only brings dangers in the life of Jaisingh, but it also provides financial stability. After a successful career as a journalist, Jaisingh can afford servants, has a personal car, travels by plane all over the country, and stays in five-star hotels. As a successful journalist, Jaisingh gets invitations from foreign embassies. But Jaisingh does journalism for the reformation to the society. Through his journalism, he points out the dark sides of society to the public. But here, Kakasaheb makes criticism on Jaisingh for writing papers in English. The general people are not well known with English, and thus, Jaising fails to grab the attention of a large number of people. Only a small percentage of common people know English, and they can't change the system as a majority is far away from reality. Kakasaheb highlights the importance of common language in journalism to grab the attention of a large number of people. Jaisingh talks about the situation after the Press Conference, and he has decided that Kamala will be sent to the woman's home after the conference as it is a safe place for her as the police will attempt to get her in custody. Jaisingh also makes ready a lawyer for his legal action as he has done the criminal offence of buying Kamala. It is a crime in India to sell people according to the Indian Penal Code, and Jaisingh has done a crime. Jaisingh thinks he probably will not be sentenced as his editor will fight this case right up to the Supreme Court. Sarita does not like Jaisingh's idea to send Kamala to a woman's home, and she has sympathy for Kamala. Act I of the play concludes with the departure of Jaisingh and Kamala for the Press Conference.

Act II

The setting of the play in this act is also the drawing-room of Jaisingh's residence. The time is the night of the same day after the Press Conference. The doorbell rings, and Sarita opens the gate. Jaisingh, Jain, and Kamala enter the house after attending the Press Conference. Both Jaisingh and Jain are in drunken moods, and Jaisingh looks very pleased with himself that marks the success of his plan for the conference. Jain highly appreciates Jaisingh for his arrangement of Kamala as a witness to veil out on the inhuman racket and selling of women in the open market like cattle and the silent roles for the police and government in the society. He praises Jaisingh for the sensational news in journalism. Hearing the noise of their conversation, Kakasaheb enters the drawing-room. Here Jaisingh introduces Kakasaheb with Jain for the second time. The full name of Kakasaheb is Shivajirao Mohite. Jain informs Kakasaheb that Jaisingh has presented a terrific drama or tamasha at the Press Conference, and Kamala has played the central role in this drama. Through Jain, Vijay Tendulkar narrates all the incidents of the Press Conference. The photographers are incapable to have a good picture of Kamala for the cover pages of their newspapers. One of them asked Kamala to move her veil and show her face. Another photographer tried to get her to pose hand-in-hand with Jaisingh. Here Vijay Tendulkar portrays the nude picture of civil society. In this society, the simplicity and innocence of Kamala is run over by the crafty nature of the civil society. Kamala is an illiterate Adivasi woman, and in the Press Conference, she is among the literate men and faces their crafty and intellectual questions, which she never knows in her life. The journalists like Gupta and Chand Vaswani ask her questions on the economic exploitation of the tribal, poverty line, free sex, and illegitimate children. It seems that Kamala just has completed her degree in Economics from a reputed University, and here she faces a conference. Chand Vaswani asks Kamala a question in a threatening manner, and he wants to know from where Jaisingh bought her, and he behaved like a lawyer rather than a reporter with Kamala. Kakasaheb is a journalist, and he is well known with the morality of journalism. Hearing the incidents of the Press Conference, Kakasaheb becomes irritated as he feels that in the Press Conference the morality has been butchered. For him, it is not the right way to deal with a woman by the journalists. Kamala was the funniest object in the conference for all the journalists, and Kakasaheb considers it is wrong to laugh at the poor woman by the educated journalists who have spoiled the morality of journalism. Jaisingh intends to represent Kamala as evidence to prove the woman's auction in society. He has intended to highlight the poor quality of Adivasi life. But the situation has taken wrong way in the Press Conference. Kamala became the funniest object in the conference rather than to point out the grim system of human trafficking in society. The journalists showed their interest to humiliate Kamala and made fun of her rather than pointing out the grave problem in society. They failed to highlight the condition of the tribal society. Both Kakasahed and Sarita are bored to hear the conversation of Jain and Jaisingh about the conference. Here Vijay Tendulkar criticises the trend of journalism that violates its dignity. Kakasaheb tells Jaisingh that it is an unsuitable act that he has bought Kamala from a bazaar and sold her in the Press Conference. He criticises Jaisingh to make Kamala the funniest object for the journalists in the conference. It makes Jaisingh angry, and the atmosphere in the house of Jaisingh becomes very hot and tensed. Jaisingh has lost his balance with Kakasaheb and becomes angry with him. An uneasy silence prevails in the drawing-room. In this tense situation, Jain leaves the residence of Jaisingh and Kakasaheb goes to his room.

The next important conversation is between Kamala and Sarita. It is Kamala who is pleased with the aristocratic structure to the residence of her master, Jaisingh. She considers the bedroom of her master is in the best room in this residence. Kamala becomes shocked that in this big house, there are no children. Kamala is silly and innocent about the contemporary society in Delhi. She wants to know the price of Sarita paid by her master, Jaisingh. She thinks that Jaisingh has also bought Sarita like her. Here Sarita acts according to Kamala and informs her that she has been also bought like her by their master, Jaisingh, and for her, their master paid seven hundred rupees. Here for Kamala, Jaisingh paid two and fifty hundred, and when she comes to know that for Sarita, her master has paid seven hundred and Sarita becomes unable to have children for Jaisingh, she is surprised. Kamala considers herself as the wife or an object, and Jaisingh is her master. After knowing the information about Sarita and her price, she also considers her as an object possessed by Jaisingh. Kamala makes a plan with Sarita to make happy their master. Kamala will give birth to children as many as Sarita wants, and it is decided that Sarita will teach them and go on holidays and feast days with Jaisingh. On the other hand, she will work from morning to evening. She asks about a land possessed by Jaisingh where she can work. Thus Kamala agrees with Sarita about her domestic life, but she is ignorant of the reality of her life that she will be sent to a woman's home and can't live with them. The systems and laws of society will never allow her to live with Sarita. Here her simplicity and innocence are killed by the system of society.

Here Vijay Tendulkar brings some changes in this act. The scene of the play opens the next day morning. The time passes from morning to afternoon, then tonight, and now it is morning once again. Jaisingh reads the newspapers very seriously, which contain the news about his Press Conference. The different articles contain different information about Kamala and her price paid by Jaisingh. He greets Kakasaheb in the morning. Jaisingh receives phone calls and is greeted over the phone. The repeated calls make Jaisisngh irritated, and he at least unplugs the phone from the wall connection and goes upstairs and asks Sarita to send tea there for him. Kakasaheb tells Sarita that he wants to leave for his home that day, and hearing the news of the departure of Kakasaheb, Sarita becomes upset and requests him not to leave that day. Kakasaheb tells Sarita to remind Jaisingh to contact the Secretary about his quota of newspaper for his magazine. Sarita thinks that Kakasaheb is leaving because of the rude conduct by Jaisingh at the previous night. Sarita begins to cry and tells him to stay with them at least for that day, and Kakasaheb changes his decision to return home and he assures her that he will stay. Jaisingh comes down from upstairs and reconnects the plug with the phone. He rebukes Kamalabai and tells her to arrange the papers properly on the rack. He asks Kamalabai to tell Kamala to be ready and do it very quickly. Jaisingh wants to send her to the woman's house and asks Kamala to get ready for it. The phone rings again, and it is a call from Neeti Bagh police station and asks for Jaisingh. It becomes clear that an F.I.R has been lodged against Jaisingh for his act of buying Kamala. Jaisingh avoids the call and becomes hasty for Kamala to send her to the woman's home. The call from the Neeti Bagh police station creates an unrest situation in the residence of Jaisingh for all. Jaisingh's buying is a criminal offence according to the Indian Penal Code, and the police want the custody of Kamala. Kamala enters wearing a sari of Sarita, who seems to be unwilling to leave the house, and at the same time, Sarita also asks Jaisingh not to send Kamala to the woman's home, and she should stay with them. Both Sarita and Jaisingh are arguing about Kamala. Jaisingh says that Kamala must go to the woman's home, but Sarita says Kamala must stay with them. He has performed a crime of buying Kamala, and to escape from the punishment and win the case, Kamala must go to the woman's home. In this regard, Jaisingh clarifies to Sarita that only Jaisingh has the authority to take decisions in this house, and nobody, even Sarita, is allowed to take decisions in this house. Such bold speech by Jaisingh shakes the spirit of Sarita. At least Jaisingh leaves with Kamala for the woman's home.

Here once again, Vijay Tendulkar has brought a change in this act. The time moves, and the action shifts from morning to evening. In the morning, Jaising has left the house with Kamala for the woman's home, and in the evening, he returns to his residence. But on the other hand, Sarita has lost her harmony as she has been told that she has no authority to take decisions on any subjects in this house and must act according to her husband. It has shaken her as she always considers that she has the authority in this house. Jaisingh returns home after leaving Kamala to the woman's house and asks Kamalabai to inform Sarita to get ready for the party. He has informed Kamalabai to deliver a message to his wife to get ready for the evening party before returning to the house. At seven in the evening, they will go to the party, but Sarita is not dressed for the party, and she is still wearing her morning clothes, and she has been staying in her room from the morning. Sarita is upset with the conduct of her husband. Jaisingh asks her to get ready, but Sarita asks him about Kamala, who is now in a woman's home. Jaisingh makes a call to the Press Club and informs Chadda about his probable journey to Andhra to next day to cover a report of police firing on an assembly of Gond tribe members. In this firing, nine or ten people were killed. After a grim conversation with his wife, Sarita, Jaisingh leaves his residence without Sarita. Kakasaheb, who has gone out in the afternoon, returns to the residence of Jaisingh after the existence of Jaisingh in the evening. Sarita expresses her wish about a Press Conference at her uncle, where she wants to expose Jaisingh. At this conference, all journalists in Delhi must come, and in front of them, Sarita wants to expose her husband, Jaisingh, and his duel characters. He seems to be liberal and advocates for freedom for the general people through his writings on paper, but Jaisingh is himself a keeper of a slave. According to Sarita, Jaisingh brings home a slave and exploits her, and he tyrannises his slave as much as he likes. Sarita considers herself a slave for Jaisingh after her controversy with her husband about Kamala, and it becomes clear for her that she has nothing important in the life of Jaisinigh and in his family to take a decision. There is no difference between Kamala and Sarita as both are forced to accept the decision of Jaisingh. Sarita is the wife of Jaisingh, and Kamala is his slave, but Jaisingh never shows too much affection for Sarita. She thinks that Kamala breaks her sleep and wakes her up from the sleep to perceive reality. For Kamala, it becomes clear of Sarita. She considers Jaisingh as her life partner, but he is the master of her life, and she is a slave for him. As a slave, she has no right in the house. Kakasaheb hears Sarita and her objection to the rules in domestic life. He attempts to console her that Jaisingh is not a different person and he is like other behaves like usual. Here Sarita asks about women empowerment in society. She wants to know the reasons behind the suppression of women in society and not living like a man. A woman can do everything as a man can, and a man has no extra sense from a woman, yet this discrimination is still in society. In the middle of their conversation on the subject of women's empowerment in society and the family, the doorbell rings. It is Jain who comes from the Press Club to deliver the sad news to the family. He informs that for the Press Conference with Kamala, Jaisingh becomes a target for some big and powerful people, and under the pressure of these people, Jaisingh is sacked from his service by his boss. That news shocks everyone in this family. Kakasaheb considers it as an injustice for Jaisingh, a bold journalist who has disclosed the flesh racket in society. Sarita makes a call, and after some time, Jaisingh returns to his residence and comes to know the incident. It is decided that Jaisingh would receive his dismissed letter from his boss the next day, and the decision has been taken after a high-level meeting. Jaisingh wants to contact his editor, but his editor has taken a plane for Bombay. He rebukes his boss, Sheth Singhania, for such a rusty decision and scolds him in dirty language. Jaisingh becomes wild with the news of his dismiss from the job, and Kakasaheb suggests legally fighting against this injustice, and the owner will change his decision for Jaisingh in court. Jaisingh loses his self-control and collapses onto the sofa. Jain leaves the residence of Jaisingh. The news of the dismissal of Jaisingh from his job has interrupted Sarita to think about the woman's empowerment, but when Jaisingh sleeps on the sofa, she again talks about the same thing and assures her uncle, Kakasaheb, that one day she will be free from the slavery and she will no longer be an object to be used and thrown away. The act of the play concludes with the hope of Sarita and her liberty from the clutches of Jaisingh. It is night, and Kakasaheb slowly goes to his room, and Sarita turns off the lights in the drawing-room one by one, leaving just one light on. She comes close to Jaisingh and sits on the ground by the sofa, her head against it. She closes her eyes, exhausted, and opens them again. Thus the Act II of the play concludes.

Critical Appreciation

Setting

The play, *Kamala*, sets in the modern Indian society in New Delhi. The residence of Jaisingh Jadhav in Neeti Bagh is the setting of the play. All the actions are performed in the drawing-room of this residence. Here Jaisingh lives with his wife, Sarita, and their maid, Kamalabai. Sarita's uncle, Kakasaheb, has come to Delhi to collect printing paper for his magazine, and he stays in the residence of Jaisingh. All the actions of the play, *Kamala*, are performed within two days. It is a short play about two acts. Some actions of play are not performed; they are informed. The Press Conference is not acted, and it is informed.

Title

Vijay Tendulkar titled this play on the name of its central character, Kamala. She is a tribal or Adivasi woman, and she is a criticism to contemporary Indian civil society. The primary themes of the play are the auction of women in open markets, and the silent roles of police and government. In the states like Bihar, the women are openly sold in the bazaar, and this inhuman flesh racket is controlled by some powerful big people. Kamala is presented as a witness to the civil society to disclose this inhuman bazaar. Kamala influences the domestic life of Sarita, who considers herself as the partner to her husband, Jaisingh. Kamala puts down the veil for the eyes of Sarita that she is not the partner of her husband, but she is also a slave like her, and Jaisnigh is her master. Here Vijay Tendulkar has used an apt and appropriate title for his play, *Kamala*. It is a socialist play that talks about the social reformation in India in the modern period. The play has pointed out living qualities to the Indian tribal society or Adivasi society. It is a play about gender discrimination, and here Vijay Tendulkar shows it through Kamala. It is found between Kamala and literate civil society in India. Kamala is humiliated in the Press Conference by literate journalists because she is a woman and belongs to the tribal society. In this play, *Kamala*, Vijay Tendulkar compares the simplicity of tribal society with the complexity of literate society through the central character Kamala.

Journalism

The *Kamala* is a play on the role of journalism in society. Here Vijay Tendulkar explains bold and good journalism, and at the same time, he attempts to point out its faults and shortcomings. Both Kakasaheb and Jaisnigh are journalists. Kakasaheb is old, and when he was young, he wrote against the British imperial role in India. He fought for Indian liberation with his pen and was imprisoned for his bold spirit. The bravery and boldness are the common characters of journalists, and a successful true journalist is identified with his brave and bold spirit in writing. Kakasaheb is a true journalist. Jaisingh is also a brave journalist, and he is known for his bold activities. He has disclosed the inhuman flesh racket in post-independent India. He bought a tribal woman, Kamala, as a witness to put down the veil of the society. Here Vijay Tendulkar also points out the changes in the history of journalism in India. In colonised India, journalists like Kakasaheb wrote for society and criticised the government and its systems, but journalists like Jaisingh write for the sensational news in post-independent India. Journalism becomes a field of the race for sensational news rather than focusing on reforming society. In this play, the basic intention to buy Kamala is to create sensational news in the world of journalism. He is a bold journalist, but he has some shortcomings. The reformation in the tribal society and the development of the quality of living of the Adivasi women like Kamala are excluded in Jaisingh's Press Conference. Vijay Tendulkar also points out the life of a journalist. For this profession, they are always targeted and threatened to be killed. Kakasaheb, for his journalism, was imprisoned, and now, for his brave spirit, Jaisnigh receives threatening calls. But the difference is that at the time of Kakasaheb, the enemy was open, and now for Jaisingh, the enemy is hidden and unidentified. At the same time, for the sensational news of Kamala in the Press Club, Jaisingh has been sacked from his job. Here Vijay Tendulkar shows the importance of language in journalism. He thinks that the papers should be written in dialect so that a large number of people can read them. Kakasaheb tells Jasingh that his paper is read by a minor group of people as it is written in English.

Tribal Society and Literate Society

The *Kamala* is a play that compares the simplicity and innocence of the tribal or Adivasi society with the complexity and crafty nature of literate and civil society. Kamala symbolises the innocence and simplicity of the Adivasi society that is mocked by the literate and educated people at the Press Club during the Press Conference. Kamala, a tribal woman, has been bought by Jaisingh as a witness for sensational news for his newspaper to open the cye of society on the subjects of human trafficking and flesh racket. He arranges a Press Conference for this sensational and grave subject. But in the Press Conference, Kamala becomes the funniest object for all the journalists and laughs at her. Here Kamala's simplicity has been butchered by the complexity of literate civil society. In this conference, she has been asked questions on economics, free sex, illegitimate children, and the poverty line. Such questions should be asked to an expert, not to an ignorant woman like Kamala. Kamala takes Jaisingh as her master and husband, but she is totally blind to the reality of her life in Delhi that Jaisingh uses her as a tram card for his career, and she is nothing special for him rather than the sensational news. She wishes to live in the residence of Jaisingh, but she is sent to a woman's home.

Woman's Empowerment

The *Kamala* is a play that talks about the woman's empowerment in the domestic life. Sarita is the devoted wife of Jaisingh, and she considers him as her life partner. She thinks of herself as the mistress of the house. It is Kamala who opens her eyes that Sarita is also a slave for Jaisingh. The difference is that Sarita is a domestic slave for Jaisngh, and she maintains his domestic life, whereas Kamala is a slave for his career as a journalist. Jaisingh clarifies to Sarita that he is the master of the house and nobody can take decision in the family when he decides to send Kamala to the woman's house. Sarita possesses a revolutionary spirit, and she wants to arrange a Press Conference to disclose her husband. She wants to disclose Jaisingh as a slave master. Through Kakasaheb, Vijay Tendulkar clarifies that in every family, man is the master, and woman is under his domination. Sarita is dominated by her husband, but in every family, there are many women like Sarita, who are also dominated by their husbands. At the end of the play, through Sarita, Vijay Tendulkar prophesies the equality between man and woman, and it concludes with the subject of woman's empowerment in society.

Characters

Kamala

She is the titled character in the play. She is a tribal woman, and she comes to New Delhi with Jaisingh, who has bought her from a flesh market in Bihar for two hundred and fifty rupees. She is known for the simplicity and innocence of life. Kamala considers Jaisingh as her master, and she is an obedient creature to her master. Kamala is presented as a witness to prove the flesh racket in the society at the

Press Conference by Jaisingh, but she becomes the funniest object for all the journalists. Her simplicity is mocked by the complexity of civil society. She makes an agreement with Sarita to please their master, Jaisingh. She will give birth children as many as Sarita needs, and Kamala wants to work in the land of Jaisingh from morning to evening. The influence of Kamala is clearly noticed in Sarita. After the departure of Kamala for the woman's home, Sarita wants to arrange a Press Conference against her husband, Jaisingh. Kamala takes the residence of Jaisimgh as a palace, and she is pleased with it and prefers to live with Jaisingh and Sarita.

Jaisingh Jadhav

He is a journalist and works for an English newspaper. He lives with his wife, Sarita, in New Delhi. He is brave and bold as a journalist and dares to write against an M. P., and he receives threatening phone calls, but Jaisingh takes these calls casually. The primary motive of this play is based on his sensational news. He has bought Kamala, a tribal woman, as a witness to put down the veil from the society regarding the flesh racket. He arranges a Press Conference where he produces Kamala as a witness to the civil society to prove the presence of the inhuman flesh markets in Bihar. At the end of the play, he has been shacked and dismissed from his service as a journalist for his bold act in journalism. Jaisingh is the master of his family, and it is he, who can only take a decision in his family. He has committed a criminal offence through his buying Kamala and to save himself from the penalty, Jaisingh sends Kamala to the woman's house. He takes this decision against the wills of his wife, Sarita, and Kamala. It is a Sarita at the end of this play who wants to disclose the dominant nature of Jaisingh through organising a Press Conference.

Sarita

Sarita is the wife of Jaisingh Jadhav and lives with her husband in New Delhi. She faces a problem with language in Delhi as she rattles off Hindi and Panjabi. She is a housewife, and she looks after Jaisingh and their family. She records all the phone calls in the absence of her husband. Sarita does not like that Kamala should live in the woman's home. Kamala opens her eyes that she is not a partner of Jaisisingh, but Jaisingh is her master. Sarita wants to organise a Press Conference to prove Jaisingh as the master of slaves. Sarita has deep sympathy for Kamala and wishes that Kamala should live with them.

Kakasaheb

Kakasaheb is an aged journalist, and he runs a magazine. He has come to Delhi to collect paper for his magazine and stays at the residence of his niece, Sarita, and her husband, Jaisingh. Kakasaheb is a follower of Gandhism and leads a simple life. He advises Jaisningh and Sarita for pre-conscious about the threatening phone calls. He was imprisoned as a journalist for fighting against British Rule for the liberation of India. He does not like Jaisingh's idea to buy Kamala and present her as a witness to prove the presence of the flesh racket in India.

2

Silence! The Court is in Session

Silence! The Court is in Session is a play of three acts by Vijay Tendulkar, and it is a masterpiece work in his career as a playwright. Here Vijay Tendulkar shows his craftsmanship for mixing fancy with reality. It is a play based on subjects of infanticide and motherhood. Vijay Tendulkar criticises to the elite and patriarch society and its dogmatic ideas for unmarried birth of children in post-independent India.

Summary

Act I

The play opens in a completely empty hall of a village, and this hall is used generally to celebrate functions like weddings, speeches, receptions, and bhajan. Here all the cultural functions of the village are organised. It has two doors, one to enter by and another to go to an adjoining room. Within the hall, there are a built-in platform, one or two old wooden chairs, an old box, a stool, and sundry other things lie jumbled together as if in a lumber-room. It also contains an out of order clock and some worn-out portraits of national leaders. A drama troop from Bombay is going to perform a mock law trial tonight in this hall. The Soner Moti Tenement Progressive Association is the troop from Bombay that will perform a mock trial in this hall for the villagers. The members of this troop come one after another from the railway station. Miss Leela Benare and Samant enter to the hall. Samant is a village man and he guides to Miss Leela Benare, who is an actress to the Bombay drama troop from station to the hall. They walk fast from the railway station, and they leave behind others and come fast to the hall. Miss Leela Benare is an unmarried open-minded woman, and she talks very frankly to Samant. The frankness of Benare embraces Samant. He is a bachelor, and he has a green clothe of parrot for his nephew, and Benare thinks this parrot perhaps belongs to the wife of Samant. He informs about the cultural functions in this hall, and recently he has attended magic shows, and Benare asks him if he has seen any show of cutting tongue and putting it together again. They are alone in the hall, and Miss Leela Benare seduces him, and she comes very close to Samant, who tries to keep his distance from her. They are waiting for the arrival of other members of the drama troop who walk slowly from the station to the hall. The conversation between Samant and Miss Leela Benare is most important as it focuses on the bachelor life of Samant, Benare's lusty character, and the value of the hall to sustain the village's cultural heritage. Miss Leela Benare shares her experience as a teacher. She is a devoted teacher, and in the classes, she is standing while teaching as she never sits when she takes classses. Her class is scared stiff of her, and she wants the last drop of her blood to teach the students who adore her and are ready to do anything for her. Benare is a liberated woman and prefers to do according to her wishes. She sings a song in the presence of Samant in the hall. Both Benare and Samant are discussing the subject of the night show for the villagers. A mock court trial will be performed for the villagers, and the hall will be a courtroom for the show. The trial is for the accused President Johnson for producing atomic weapons. Benare talks about chairman Kashikar, his wife, Mrs Kashikar, and Balu Rokde. They are also coming to perform in the night show. Balu Rokde was educated by Mr and Mrs Kashikar, and they gave him shelter. The other members are near the hall, and both Benare and Samant hide behind the door leading outside. Benare and Samant leap out from behind the door as they come in, and she shouts 'Boo' to surprise them. Sukhatme asks her to behave like a grown-up for this childish act, but Benare expresses her views of life, and she says that her soul is serious and she wants to enjoy every moment of life. She is a living woman, and she wants to utilise every moment and every bit of her life. Here Vijay Tendulkar presents brief descriptions of all the members of the troop. Sukhatme is a lawyer, Ponkshe is a science student, and Balu Rokde is the Mock Law-court's general factotum. Sukhatme presents a beautiful sketch of the character of Ponkshe. He is looked very impressive during the trial. He is a scientist in the witness box, and has completed his Inter-Science for the second time. Ponkshe works as a clerk in the Central Telegraph Office. Such presentation to the character of Ponkshe makes lough Balu Rokde who is also criticised by Ponkshe as he has received his education on Mrs Kashikar's charity. Miss Benare is open and charming, but she informs that as a child, she was different, and she was very quiet, sat and made plans, and cried very loudly. Here Vijay Tendulkar portrays the childhood and womanhood of Miss Leela Benare. She shares with them her student life, and she used to cover every book with a nice fresh cover, and the first page contained some lines with beautiful tiny letters with pictures of flowers and things. Benare recites a lyric in the hall, and Rokde attempts to write down her recitation, but she guides him like a teacher on how to write it down. As a teacher, she always tells the girls in the class not to hurry to write down what they have hardly heard. She advises them to listen first and then say it yourself slowly and send it deep inside them. Miss Leela Benare recites a Marathi poem of Mrs Shirish Pai and all assist to the rhythm of her singing. At that point, the experimental theatre actor, Karnik, enters the hall. He is chewing a pan. Karnik looks around the hall, and Sukhatme suggests that a hall is ideal for the Intimate Theatre, but Karnik considers the hall a real court. Rokde wants to know about Mr and Mrs Kashikar, who are yet to reach, and Karnik informs that they are late as Mr Kashikar wants to buy garland for his wife's hair. In this hall, they are gathering to perform a show of the Court's trial against a case of President of Johnson for producing atomic weapons. Karnik asks Rokde to check mike's batteries because they have a bad experience with it in the middle of the performance of an ordinary amateur play for Ganapati Puja. Miss Leela Benare asks Samant for some chairs. He leaves the hall and re-enters with some chairs. Now Mr and Mrs Kashikar enter the hall.

Mr Kashikar is the responsible chairman, and he wants to know from Balu Rokde that he has brought all required things for their performance as he has a habit of forgetting something to bring. Mr Kashikar asks for his judge's wig used during the trial by him as a judge. He also asks Sukhatme about his lawyer's gown as Sukhatme plays the role of a lawyer. Ponkshe informs them that he has not forgotten anything as he has come fully dressed. All in the hall look around and plan to decorate it as a court room for the trial. Sukhatme and Karnik are talking about the presentation of theatre, and here Vijay Tendulkar presents his own reviews on traditional old fashioned and modern theatres. Professor Damle, another troop member, is yet to come, and he has missed the train. It is found that Professor Damle will be incapable of coming there before the show because there is hardly any train coming before the show to the village.

Professor Damle informed Mrs Kashikar that he wouldn't be able to catch their train and he was busy in university with a symposium or something, and he assured that he will come by next train that never comes before nine p.m. It is a problem for all to manage an actor to perform his role. In the trial, Professor Damle plays the role of the counsel of defence for the accused, whereas Sukhatme plays the role of the counsel of offence. Sukhatme decides to play both roles as a counsel of defence and a council of offence. Thus the problem of Professor Damle is solved. But for them, another problem is waiting. Rawte is sick with flu, and he plays the role of the fourth witness in the trial. It is decided that Samant, the village man, would play the role of Rawte as the fourth witness for today's Living Law-court, but Samant has nothing experience about the courtroom and trial. The two actors are absent from the show, and Sukhatme will play the role of Professor Damle as a counsel of defence for the accused, and Samant also will play the role of Rawte as the fourth witness. They have enough time for the show at night, and Samant has nothing experience about the courtroom and trial; it is Mrs Kashikar, who suggests to all to have a practice trial or rehearsal so that Samant will be taught and as well as they can pass the time for the final time of the show. All agree with her. Miss Leela Benare has a habit of passing the time through reading books, but unfortunately, she has nothing to read. Here Vijay Tendulkar has used the technique 'play within play'. In this play, a drama troop comes to a village to perform a night show for the villagers, and there is much time for the final show. To pass the time and to teach Samant about the court trial, they decide to play a practice trial; thus, Vijay Tendulkar presents the setting 'play within play'. Miss Leela Benare says that they have performed the atomic weapons trial seven times in the past three months, and tonight, it will be performed for eighth time. She has no abjection doing it for another time before the night show. Sukhatme proposes a new imaginary case for the rehearsal to make Samant familiar with the trial system. All agree with him, and Karnik, a specialist in theatre, considers it as a Visual Enactment in Drama Theory. After a discussion, they have decided Miss Leela Benare was the accused of the rehearsal, and they decorate the hall to look like a courtroom. She has been accused under Section No 302 of the Indian Penal Code on the charge of infanticide. The first act of the play ends with the charge of infanticide on Benare for the practice trial. In this act, Vijay Tendulkar introduces all his characters and their arrival in a village to perform a night show for the villagers. To pass the time and teach Samant, a village man, about the court trial, they arrange a practice trial for him, and in this practice trial, Miss Leela Benare is charged with an imaginary case of infanticide.

Act II

There are no changes in the setting of Act II from the previous act. The situation is also the same as at the end of Act I. Benare is accused with the crime of infanticide. In this Act, Vijay Tendulkar shows how the imaginary charge for the rehearsal becomes very serious. Here Tendulkar shows the transformation in the atmosphere in the hall from imaginary to reality, from frivolous to serious, and he explains how the trivial and imaginary charge transforms to a serious charge for Miss Leela Benare. Mr Kashikar is the judge, Sukhatme plays the role of the counsel of offence and the counsel of defence; all the remaining members in the hall, including the village man, Samant, play the role of witness to prove Miss Benare as a culprit. Thus the setting for rehearsal is started to teach Samant about the court trial. Samant brings masala pan, beedis and cigarettes for all, and they take it. Samant is unknown about the crime of infanticide, and Sukhatme tells him it is a crime killing a new-born child and he is shocked for such a serious charge to Miss Benare. Samant says that such crimes are regularly committed in his village. So infanticide is a common crime in Indian villages that are highlighted here by Vijay Tendulkar. Sukhatme is the lawyer in the rehearsal and begins to interrogate Benare in clever ways.

At the very beginning of the trial, all are interested in spitting out the pans from their mouths rather than the trial. Sukhatme requests Kashikar, the judge in the trial, for adjournment of a quarter minute in the beginning so that they may spit out the pan from their mouths. After it, Mr Kashikar, as the judge, asks Sukhatme who plays the role of counsel of offence to present his plea in the matter of Leela Benare's crime of infanticide. Much of the Court's time has been wasted on the subject of spiting of the pan. Mrs Kakhikar informs Samant that one needs permission to speak in the Court and suggests him to watch the trial seriously. As a judge, Mr Kashikar orders all to maintain silence in the Court, and he asks Miss Leela Benare about the crime she has committed. As an accused in the rehearsal, Miss Benare wants to change the subject of trial, and she prefers the subjects like snatching the public property rather than the infanticide. But her apple doesn't work on the members of the hall, and the trial is continued. Mrs Kashikar thinks that there is nothing to worry about the present trial as it is an imaginary charge, and the trial is a rehearsal to provide Samant some experience about the trial in the Court as he is going to act as the fourth witness in the night show. Miss Leela Benare doesn't take the Court very seriously, and she denies the charge of infanticide and assures the Court that she has never even killed a common cockroach. As a lawyer, the trial moves forward, and Sukhatme provides a long speech on the importance of motherhood and the crime of infanticide. Motherhood is a sacred thing, and a mother weaves a magic circle with her complete existence to protect and preserve her little one. According to Sukhatme woman is a wife for a moment but a mother forever. Samant watches their acting, and he becomes pleased with the trial system of the Court. To prove Benare as guilty, as a lawyer of offence, Sukhatme presents his first witness Mr Gopal Ponkshe. It is a custom in the Court that the witness takes an oath before questioning. Here a dictionary is used as the Geeta for taking oath for Ponkshe. In the Court, Ponkshe provides some light on the character of Miss Leela Benare. She is a teacher, and a schoolmarm. She is unmarried in public life, according to Ponkshe, and thus he hints at some immoral, illicit nature of Benare. She is a bit too much for him, and he tries to say that Miss Benare runs after men too much. Thus the trial gradually becomes serious, and an imaginary crime becomes a real for Miss Leela Benare. The counsel Sukhatme asks Ponkshi if accused has any close relationship with any man-married or unmarried. To give light on the character of Benare, Ponkshe shares an incident that Miss Benare once tried to arrange a marriage for him.

The counsel Sukhatme calls for his second witness, Karnik, after his questioning to Ponkshe. Karnik takes also an oath to tell the truth, and he informs the Court that he comes to know Leela through the theatre group which is now performing in this hall. Both Karnik as a witness and Sukhatme as the counsel are talking about motherhood and its noble duty in society. Karnik is also asked questions to disclose the life of Miss Benare, and he says that it is Balu Rokde who has seen some compromising situations in the life of Miss Benare. After Karnik, the counsel Sukhatme calls for his third witness, Balu Rokde. He comes into the witness box, but he is puzzled and tense. His body is full with sweat. Miss Benare mocks him for such an abnormal condition, and after gathering courage, Balu speaks out the truth of Benare's life. He informs the Court that once he went to Professor Damle in the college hostel and noticed Miss Leela Benare was there. As a counsel, Sukhatme enforces Balu to say it in detail. Here the rehearsal comes up on the top level when the imaginary trial is pushed towards reality. The trail enters the personal life of Benare from the imaginary charge of infanticide. Mr Kashikar says that the trial is getting onto too personal level in the life of Miss Benare and wants to stops it here, but Sukhatme says it is just for the practice trial and it doesn't belong to the personal life of Miss Benare, who asks to the Court that there is no need to drag her private life in this trial, and she deals not only Professor Damle, but also there are twenty-five more people with whom she is alone at times. Rokde informs the Court that they were setting, and Damle got rid of him. Sukhatme asks the Court to record the point that Miss Benare was noticed to sit with Professor Damle alone, and it is a suspicious situation in the trial. For such charges, Benare becomes unrest and informs to the Court that a little while ago, she was alone with Samant and asks the Court to write it down. Samant wakes up suddenly in confusion and says that Miss Benare behaved in a most exemplary manner, and they talked about the magic shows and hypnotism. The trial seems to be a bit interesting to all, and Sukhatme is told to continue the trial. Here the personal life of Miss Benare is attempted to disclose publicly under the name of practice trial for Samant. The private life of Miss Benare becomes a topic for entertainment for all. After Balu Rokde, the counsel Sukhatme asks for his fourth witness, Samant, to prove the crime of Miss Benare. Samant has not seen a court trial, and he has no experience as a witness, so he seems to be tensed to face the questions of Sukhatme. Mrs Kashikar tells him not to worry as it is a rehearsal and it is a practice trial, not a real one. Samant takes an oath, to tell the truth, the whole truth. He says that he doesn't know well to Benare as he has met her just two hours before and it is not enough time to know one well. During the trial session, Miss Leela Benare seems to have fallen asleep. Vijay Tendulkar as a dramatist at this point has used a complex technique to provide a turning point in the play. Samant is a village man, and he does not know Miss Leela Benare; he had met with her just few hours ago, and now as a witness, Samant informs that he has seen Miss Benare with Professor Damle. Here he continues Balu Rokde and his information who has already told in the Court about the meeting between Benare and Damle. As Samant is informed that it is a practice trial and not a real one, he begins to assist as a witness to prove the crime of infanticide done by Miss Leela Benare. Samant doesn't know Professor Damle, but he says that he knows Damle and his relation with Miss Benare. Thus all the characters in the hall are united in humiliating and proving to Miss Leela Benare. Vijay Tendulkar as a dramatist, very craftily has mixed reality with fancy, and it becomes impossible for one to demark the line between imagination and reality. Here Samant shows his skill as an actor. He is trained to act as the fourth witness in the night show, and like a professional actor, he has mixed up fancy with reality. He does not know much about Miss Leela Benare and Professor Damle, but to make the practice trial interesting, he assists others in proving Benare's infanticide. He tells the Court that he has gone to the house of Professor Damle to arrange a lecture. He rang the doorbell, and the door was opened, but it was slammed to close. He didn't talk properly with Professor, but he heard a cry inside the room. It was a woman who was crying. Samant heard that the woman told Professor about her wretched condition if she had been abandoned because she has nowhere to go. But according to Samant, Professor Damle denied responsibility of this woman for his reputation in society, and the woman informed Damle that she had no choice but to take her life off. She assured Professor that she would suicide and would destroy two lives as she was pregnant. Such information about the personal life of Professor Damle by Samant changes the atmosphere in the hall. In the trial, Benare and her private life are hunted by all to make the trial interesting. Miss Leela Benare objects to Samant for his fictional story about his visit to Professor Damle, but in the hall, all show their interest in Samant and his information, and he continues it. Here charming mood of Benare changes to gloomy and angry; she begins to cry and wants to quit the trial. She picks up her bag and purse and walks towards the door to open it, but unfortunately, it is not opened as it is locked from outside. In such a critical condition, Kashikar suggests continuing the trial. Act II concludes with the tragic situation of Miss Leela Benare.

Act III

This act opens in the same scene, and the cast is in the positions they were as at the end of the second act. Sukhatme as a professional counsel asks accused Benare to come in the witness box who wants to quit the trial and attempts to leave the hall, but she is unwilling to enter the witness box as she is emotionally wounded with the information of Samant and others for her relation with Professor Damle. It is Mrs Kashikar who pushes her to the witness box to continue the trial. The charming mood of Miss Leela Benare is lost in this act, whereas in the previous acts, it is noticed that she likes to enjoy life with fun, but her fun and childish manners are killed by all who attempt to prove her to have an immoral sexual relation with Professor Damle and has done infanticide. All in the hall are excited to continue the trial. Sukhatme, as a counsel of offence, continues his questions, but Miss Benare doesn't give him any answers to his questions. Sukhatme asks her about her age, but Benare remains silent. Sukhatme also wants to know the reasons behind her unmarried life and her refusal for marriage. But Benare is still silent. Mrs Kashikar thinks that Benare may be thirty two years old. Benare avoids the questions and leaves the witness box, and goes to the door. But the door is locked from outside; Ponkshe blocks the way, she turns aside, and by then, Mrs Kashikar has hold of her and leads her to the dock. Sukhatme calls Mrs Kashikar in the witness box and asks her how Miss Leela Benare remains unmarried till such a late age. As a witness, Mrs Kashikar talks about child marriage during her time and compares it with the late marriage at the present time. There was not much freedom for the women in the society in early age, and they had to marry in their childhood, but at the present time, women like Miss Leela Benare live an unmarried life till their late age. Mrs Kashikar also talks about the responsibility and irresponsibility in life, and she wants to say that women like Miss Leela Benare are irresponsible in the present age. She also considers the system of the society that a woman can get everything without marriage. It means that a woman in the present day has financial security and sexual satisfaction without marriage. Here Mrs Kashikar wants to say that

Miss Leela Benare, by profession is a teacher and that provides her financial security, and with Professor Damle, she also satisfies her sexual urge. For Mrs Kashikar, the character of Miss Leela Benare is a mysterious one, and she doubts her for several reasons such as her unmarried life, her loud laughing, her free and frank nature, her jokes, songs, dances, and wondering alone with men. Benare is a free bird, and in the practice trial, her freedom and liberty are trapped by all. In the Court as a witness, Mrs Kashikar shares an incident, happened in September when she and her husband noticed Banare with Damle. She and her husband, Kashikar, offered to her a lift to drop her home as she was to go home alone, but Miss Leela Benare very slyly went off with Professor Damle. Damle is a family man with five children, and Miss Leela Benare has illicit relation with him. After Mrs Kashikar, Sukhatme calls for Balu Rokde as his next witness to prove the crime of Benare. Rokde informs the Court about an incident eight days ago when they were at a show at Dombivil. He was seduced by Benare, and Rokde denied her. He also slapped her for her seduction. After Balu Rokde, Ponkshe is called for once again in the witness box. Ponkshe informs that Miss Benare kept a battle of Tik-20 in her purse. It is a powerful poison, and it indicates that she may attempt suicide. Ponkshe informs the Court that he had found it out when he met with her in the Udipi restaurant where Miss Benare expressed her desire to marry him as she is pregnant and wants to save her reputation in society and the life of her child. Benare breaks her silence and cries out that Ponkshe says lie in the Court. After Ponkshe, Karnik comes into the witness box, and he informs that he has watched the meeting between Balu Rokde and Miss Leela Benare, and he says that Balu didn't slap Benare. He also criticises the parasite life of Balu Rokde. Karnik provides precious information about an incident of the past life of Miss Leela Benare. He met a cousin of accused Benare at a cricket match at the Dadar Gymkhana and was told that Benare had attempted suicide. She fell in love at the age of fifteen with her own maternal uncle, and Benare attempted suicide because of the disappointment in love. Karnik leaves the witness box; on the other hand, Miss Benare also wants to escape from the trial, and she moves towards to door, and Mrs Kashikar brings her to the dock. Mr Kashiskar is the judge in the practice trial, but he now plays the role as a witness. He comes to the witness box, and Sukhatme begins to interrogate him. Mr Kashikar as a witness considers Benare as a sinful canker on the body of society. He is a social worker, and he often visits Bombay to meet the famous leader Nanasaheb Shinde. He is also a social worker and the chairman of the Education Society. Mr Kashikar comes to know that a schoolmistress visits regularly to Shinde and wants him to drop an enquiry against her for her unmarried pregnancy. Mr Kashikar shares an incident that once she noticed to talk Nanasaheb Shinde angrily over the phone to dismiss a mistress from her service for her unmarried pregnancy. All information relate to Miss Benare, her relation with Professor Damle, and her pregnancy before the marriage. At that point, a small battle is in Benare's hand, and she is about to put it in her mouth; Karnik dashes forward and strikes it away. The battle rolls towards Ponkshe's feet, and it is Tik-20.

Now there are some changes in the trial are noticed. Here Sukhatme has changed his role as a counsel of defence. He is now the counsel of the accused of Benare to defend all the charges and prove her innocence. The witnesses from the side of accused Benare are Professor Damle, Nanasaheb Shinde, and Mr Rawte. But all witnesses are absent in the Court, and it becomes impossible to defend the charges against Miss Leela Benare. As the counsel of the defence, Sukhatme wants to cross-examine the witnesses presented in the Court, but Kashikar, as judge, denies this appeal of Sukhatme. Now Sukhatme becomes once again the counsel for the prosecution from the counsel for accused Benare. As the counsel for the prosecution, Sukhatme gives a lecture at the end of the trial. He says that Miss Leela Benare is truly dreadful, and she has made a heinous blot on the sacred brow of the motherhood, which is purer than heaven itself. Unmarried motherhood is a great sin by religion and tradition, and infanticide is a dreadful act, according to Sukhatme as the counsel for the prosecution. He considers it as a horrifying act that bringing up the child of an illegal union. He also talks about the role of the women in society to build up high value in society. But the liberty of women causes unmarried pregnancy in the society that destroys the high value of the society, so the women are not fit for liberty as they misuse their power of liberty. Sukhatme appeals to the Court not to show any mercy to the accused Benare and asks for the greatest and severe punishment. This is the speech by Sukhatme as the counsel for the prosecution. Sukhatme as the counsel for the accused Benare, asks for mercy for humanity's sake for Benare, as human is prone to error. Before the final judgement, Kashikar asks Benare to say something. It is a long speech by Benare at the end of the play. She comments on her silence in her life, her profession as a devoted teacher, her liberty and privacy in life. She criticises the society and its culture. Benare accepts her immoral relation with her maternal uncle and her attempt to suicide. Benare also accepts her guilty for her unmarried life and grown-up woman. She criticises the lusty eyes of man on a woman's body. At the end of the trial, Kashikar declares his judgement that there is no mercy for accused Benare of her crime of infanticide. The social customs are of supreme importance. He says that marriage is the foundation of society's stability, and motherhood must be sacred and pure. The final judgement is that Benare shall live, but the child in her womb shall be killed. Thus the rehearsal concludes. After the practice trial, Miss Leela Benare is serious and silent. The villagers come to the hall for the night show, and they open the door. All the members of the troop are preparing for the final night show.

Critical Appreciation

Setting

Silence! The Court is in Session is the masterpiece work of Vijay Tendulkar, and it is considered as one of the greatest plays in the history of Indian theatre. The play contains a unique setting. It opens in a hall of a village, and this hall is used for the cultural programmes. Here a drama troop from Bombay has come to perform a night show for the villagers. It is a court trial against President Johnson for his invention of atomic weapons. But some troop members are absent, and it is decided that a village man,

Samant, will play in the night show as the fourth witness. It is a play, where Vijay Tendulkar has used the technique of play within play. Generally it is a play about a drama troop and its arrival in a village hall for a performance. Samant is a village man, and he has nothing experience about the Court and its trial, and he will act in the night show; so the troop members decides to perform a rehearsal before the final show to teach Samant. A play is performed as a rehearsal in this play. Thus Vijay Tendulkar has employed the technique of play within play. In the practice trial, Miss Leela Benare is the culprit, and she has been accused of infanticide, whereas in the final play, President Johnson is accused of his invention of the atomic weapons. Sukhatme, in the rehearsal, plays double roles. He is the counsel for prosecution and the counsel for accused Benare. As the counsel for the prosecution, he can prove Miss Leela Benare as the culprit of the crime of infanticide, and as the counsel for the accused, Benare, fails to prove the innocence of Benare.

Title

The original title of the play is *Shantata! Court Chalu Ahe* and the title phrase has been translated to English as *Silence! The Court is in Session*. The silence must prevail in the Court at the time of trial as the chaos prevents making a perfect judgement. In this play, Vijay Tendulkar shows the importance of silence in the Court. At the very fast of the rehearsal in the Court, the silence does not prevail as culprit Miss Benare, the judge Mr Kashikar, counsel Sukhatme, and the witnesses are not serious about the trial. The silence prevails in the third act, and all prove that Miss Benare is the culprit and has committed the crime of infanticide.

Reality and Imagination

It is a play where it becomes very difficult to draw a borderline between imagination and reality. Here Vijay Tendulkar has mixed reality with fancy and imagination, so it is impossible to identify what reality is or what imagination is. Samant is a village man, and he has no experience with the Court and its trial. He meets a drama troop that has come to his village to perform a show, a court trial. Samant meets Miss Leela Benare for the first time, and he does not know her well, but as a witness, he tells a fancy story that he knows Benare and Professor Damle. The other witnesses in the practice trial present their views on Damle and Benare in such ways that it becomes very hard to distinguish reality from fancy.

Women's Liberty

It is a play about women's liberty in contemporary Indian society. Here Vijay Tendulkar has pointed out how the woman's liberty is suspiciously looked at by the majority of the society. Miss Leela Benare is a grown-up woman. She is a devoted school teacher and a liberal unmarried woman, but her unmarried liberal life has been interrogated by the society. Her unmarried life in the practice trial is identified with immoral sexual relations. Through the trial, the unmarried life is proved as a hindrance to a stable society. Sukhatme as the counsel of prosecution tells that women are not fit for liberty because they misuse their power of liberty. Vijay Tendulkar here has highly pointed out the subject of liberty for women's society. At the time of Mrs Kashikar, the women had no liberty, and they were married in their childhood. They were dependent on their family. But the time has been changed. It is a time for women like Miss Leela Benare, and they can decide their time of marriage. Here Vijay Tendulkar has pointed out the relation between child marriage and unmarried womanhood.

Motherhood and Infanticide

Vijay Tendulkar in this play *Silence! The Court is in Session* makes a comparative study between motherhood and infanticide. Motherhood is the noble and heavenly duty in any society, and this duty is violated with sin like infanticide. Miss Leela Benare is an unmarried mother, and she, in the practice trial, has been accused of the gravest crime of infanticide. It is an unpardonable crime as she supposed to kill a new-born child to hide her unmarried motherhood. In the Indian traditional civilised society, unmarried motherhood and infanticide are the gravest crimes. Benare is accused of the crime of infanticide, but such crime is also performed by the traditional patriarch society. In the final judgement, Mr Kashikar gives his judgement that Miss Leela Benare for her crime will live, but the child in her womb will not be allowed to live as this child is the dark spot in the India traditional civilised society. Like Miss Leela Benare, Mr Kashikar does the same crime through his death sentence to Benare's child. For Benare, to kill a child is a crime, but for the Court and Mr Kashikar, it is not a crime, and it becomes a judgement.

Characters

Miss Leela Benare

Miss Leela Benare is the central character of the play. She is perhaps thirty-two or thirty-four years old. Benare is an aged unmarried woman, and she is a school teacher by profession. She is a charming woman and wants to enjoy life fully. She is also an actress who has come to a village to perform a night show. Benare sings songs and recites poems, and she is an open-minded woman. In the practice trial, she has been accused of the crime of infanticide. All members of the troop prove her relation with Professor Damle to have an illegitimate child. In this play, her private life is the centre of attraction to all. In the practice court trial, she has been charged on several grounds. She is charged for her unmarried life, violating motherhood, illicit relations with Professor Damle, and murdering a baby child. Her frankness and open-minded behaviour are criticised and mocked during the rehearsal.

Samant

Samant is the village man who guides the troop from the station to the hall. Miss Leela Benare walks fast from the station, leaves behind others, and comes fast in the hall. He tells about the importance of the hall for the village's cultural life. Samant shares his experience with a magic show performed in this hall. He brings pan, bidding, and other things for the troop members. For the night trial, some members of the drama troop are absent, and it is decided that Samant will play the role of the fourth witness in the trial against the case of President Johnson for his invention of atomic weapons. But he does not have any experience in the court trial, and it is decided that a rehearsal will be performed to teach him about the court trial. Technically it is Samant for whom Vijay Tendulkar has used the 'play within play' technique in this play. In *Silence! The Court is in Session*, a practice play, or a rehearsal is performed for Samant. Practically he does not know well Miss Leela Benare and Professor Damle, but at the time of rehearsal, he informs that once he paid a visit to the house of Damle to arrange a lecture and during this time, he has noticed some suspected incidents in his house. These incidents relate to Miss Leela Benare's private life with Professor Damle.

Sukhatme

Sukhatme is a member of the drama troop who has come to a village to perform a night show. In the trial, he plays the role of counsel. In the rehearsal, Sukhatme plays the role of the counsel for prosecution and the counsel for accused Benare. As the counsel for the prosecution, he is excellent in the practice trial and enables to prove the crimes of Miss Leela Benara. He has proved that Benare is guilty in several grounds like unmarried motherhood and infanticide. He thinks that women should have no liberty because, for liberty, women destroy society's moral codes. As the counsel for accused Benare, Sukhatme fails to present a witness to defend the case. Sukhatme presents Ponkshe, Karnik, Balu Rokde, Samant, and Mr and Mrs Kashikar as the counsel for prosecution against Miss Leela Benare, but as the counsel of Benare, Sukhatme is unable to present Professor Damle and Nanasaheb Shidhe to defend the case for Benare. He is a crafty actor and knows the skill to prosecute in the Court.

Mr and Mrs Kashikar

Both Mr and Mrs Kashikar are members of the drama troop, and both play roles for the Sonar Moti Tenement Progressive

Association. In the trial, Mr Kashikar plays the role of the judge, whereas his wife plays the role of a witness. Mr Kashikar is the chairman. Mrs Kashikar pulls accused Benare to the dock or witness box at the time of rehearsal when Miss Leela Benare wants to escape from the trial. As a witness, Mrs Kashikar says that once she and her husband have caught Miss Benare with Professor Damle. She witnesses against Benare. Mr Kashikar is the judge in the practice trial, but at the end of the trial, he also witnesses against Miss Leela Benare. As a judge, Mr Kashikar gives the judgement on the crime of infanticide that Miss Leela Benare shall live, but the child in her womb shall not live. He gives a death sentence to the child, and thus he also performs the crime of infanticide.

Balu Rokde, Ponkshe, and Karnik

Balu Rokde is a man who depends on Mr and Mrs Kashikar, who educated him. He gives witness in the practice trial against Miss Leela Benare. He has pointed out that he once noticed Miss Benare in the house of Professor Damle, and such information in the trial makes the trial interesting for all. He also informs the Court that he slapped Miss Benare for her evil character with him. Ponkshe plays the role of witness in the Court. According to Sukhatme, he is the scientist in the witness box. He has taken his Inter-Science for the second time and works as a clerk in the Central Telegraph Office. As a witness, Ponkshe discloses in the Court that Miss Leela Benare carries a bottle of Tik-20. It is poison. Karnik is another member of the drama group. He is an experimental theatre actor. He also gives witness against Miss Leela Benare on the charge of the crime of infanticide. He is very conscious about the performance and asks Rokde to check the mike's batteries before their performance at night.

3

Sakharam Binder

Sakharam Binder is one of the greatest plays by Vijay Tendulkar. It is a play about gender discrimination in India. The plot relates with Sakharam Binder, a hunter of deprived women and brings them one after another in his house to maintain his domestic life and satisfy his sexual urge.

Summary

Act I

Scene I

The setting of the play is the house of Sakharan Binder. It is a red-titled house, and there are two rooms – an outer room and a kitchen with a window at the back. He is an unmarried Bharmin, but he considers himself Mahar, a lower caste in the Hindu Society. The play opens in the evening, and Sakharam enters his house, followed by a woman. The woman is Laxmi. Sakharam is middle-aged, possesses a coarse but impressive personality, and the moustaches are salt-and-pepper stubble on the chin. Sakharam is wearing a dhoti, a grimy shirt, and a jacket. Laxmi appears terrified, and she clutches a bundle held close to her bosom and cowers near the wall, trembling with fright. Sakharam is the master of the house, and he informs about the rules, which must be maintained in this house by Laxmi, who has come to live with him. He also talks about his rude nature to Laxmi. Sakharam introduces himself as hot-headed, a womanizer, a drunkard, beats people when he loses his temper, and foul-mouthed, and there is always a bidi or an oath on his lips.

Sakharam instructs her how she will live in this house. He is the master and will give her two square meals per day and two saris to start with and then once every year. There is a well at the back of this house; a lavatory is further down. But the well dries in summer, and she will have to fetch water from the river that is a mile away from the house of Sakharam. The scorpions are around the house in the monsoon. He instructs her strictly to follow his orders; otherwise, she will be thrown out from the house without mercy. If someone calls, she is not supposed to look up and talk, but she will talk briefly, covering her head to strangers at his absence. In the absence of Sakharam, she must not allow anyone to enter the house. Laxmi looks around the house, listens carefully to Sakharam, and moves to the kitchen to make tea. Sakharam is a man who talks about himself and the rules of the house. He is a Brahmin by birth, but he considers himself as Mahar, a dirty scavenger. He is unconscious about the kitchen and tells Laxmi to search for tea leaves and sugar. Sakharam is a man who brings one woman after another woman to live with him. The previous one has left the house on Friday, and she might finish the tea leaves as she used to drink a lot of tea. Laxmi is a religious woman, and she looks for the gods in this house, but Sakharam says that he does not believe in God though he belongs to the Brahmin society. He is not a saint, and he is a man, and according to him, worship and prayer can't satisfy the itch. Sakharam brought several women into his house, and every woman had a different test and possessed different characters. If one is religious, but next one is not interested in God and worship. He does not know where God is in this house, but he must be somewhere in his house. Sakharam tells about the previous woman in this house. She was attacked with T. B. and he took her to the hospital at Miraj, where she died in last Friday. The woman was devoted to her husband, who used to worship her husband's shirt rather than God, and her husband was out to kill her, and she died hugging her husband's shirt. Sakharam brings down his mridanga from a peg and begins to play it, and Laxmi brings tea for him. Dawood Miyan, a Muslim friend of Sakharam, pays a visit to the house. He is interested in the new bird of Sakharam. He informs that he has brought Laxmi from Sonavane, and he found her in a dharmshala where she was beaten and kicked in every minute of the day. Sakharam expresses the philosophy of his unmarried life, and he is happy with it as things are fine in his life. He gets everything that he wants, and yet he is not tied down. Laxmi in the kitchen and cooks dinner, finds a small oil lamp, places it in front of the gods, a bell chimes in the distance, and folds her hands in prayer. In the outer room, Sakharam and Dawood are engrossing with their ganja. Laxmi gives some coals to Sakharam to burn ganja, and they cry out 'Bam-Bhole'. The light fades, and the mridanga resounds.

Scene II

Sakharam plays the mridanga in the outer room, and Laxmi is in the kitchen. She folds her hands before the gods and then lies down on the rags, curled with her hands under her head. Sakharam stops playing the mridanga and goes out. Laxmi comes into the outer room, sweeps the floor, picks up the chilum, and puts it away. Sakharam re-enters the outer room, and she cowers in fear. Laxmi spreads out a mattress for him, but Sakharam tells her to sleep there and orders her to press his legs before he goes to sleep. All the women in the house did it before her arrival, and it is her responsibility to serve Sakharam in that way. They come and go, but the house's custom never changes, and Laxmi must maintain the custom. Sakharam asks her about her name and her husband's name. She tells her name, but she denies uttering her husband's name as it is a tradition not to utter the name of a husband by his wife. She begins to cry for her past life, her husband, but Sakharam rebukes her for the sympathy of her husband, who kicked her out of the house and squeezed the life out of her. Sakharam asks her about her dinner, but she is fasting as it is Chaturthi. Sakharam warns her not to fast in his house and tells her to eat twice a day as she will serve him. Laxmi asks for cotton to light the oil lamp before sleeping. She is a pious lady, whereas Sakharam does not pay any attention to God. He tells her that he does not know about such religious things; he knows about the chilum and the mridanga. He assures her that he would bring cotton the next day for her prayer. Sakharam informs Laxmi about the previous woman who was living with him in this house. She was the sixth woman. She was not much in bed, she just seemed to dry up, and she wasted away. She had no flesh in her body except bones and devoted to her husband. She never raised her eyes and respected Sakharam. She had two children, and her husband kept them. At the time of her death, she kept repeating her husband's name and remembered her children. Sakharam also informs Laxmi about the last right of this woman performed by him. Here Vijay Tendulkar presents the harsh reality of the domestic women.

Scene III

This scene describes the sleeping position of Sakharam and Laxmi. He is snoring away, Laxmi is by his feet, and she is sitting with her head and knees. She closes her eyes for a while, then she opens them.

Scene IV

The light comes on, and Laxmi is in the kitchen and looks less drawn and haggard now and shows her signs of life. The outer room is empty. Laxmi is talking to a black ant, and in the mean-time, Sakharam comes back from work, stands at the doorway, and listens to Laxmi. At first, he embraced with such talking of Laxmi in his house where nobody is allowed to enter during his absence. She serves tea to Sakharam, and he forces her to drink tea from his cup, but Laxmi reluctantly takes a sip from the teacup of Sakharam. She informs that in the kitchen, she is talking with a black ant. She gives sugar to that ant, and he walks very slowly and goes around the grain of sugar before putting his mouth with it. Here Sakharam makes a comparison between Laxmi and his previous woman. The previous woman, who was numbered sixth, used to hug her husband's shirt, and the present one, Laxmi, talks to ants. After drinking tea and talking about the ant, she goes to the kitchen, washes the cup and saucer, and searches for something. On the other hand, Sakharam brings his chilum and its paraphernalia from the usual niche and waits for his partner, Dawood. In the kitchen, Laxmi continues talking with the ant, and Sakhram becomes irritated with Laxmi's behaviour toward the ant and tells her to stop such a thing in his house. Here the brutality of Sakharam is noticed when he shows no sympathy for Laxmi, whose foot is roasted with the burning coals. Laxmi cries for terrible pain.

Scene V

A very dim light is in the kitchen, and the outer room is in complete darkness. Laxmi is sleeping, and Sakharam tells her to wake up, but she shows her reluctance to act according to him. Sakharam orders her to laugh as she has laughed for the ant, and now her master orders her to laugh. He threats Laxmi, and both later begin to laugh. Here Vijay Tendulkar presents the patriarch character of Sakharam and his power over the women in his house.

Scene VI

It is the time of Ganpati puja, and the shouting 'Mangalmurti Morya' is heard from the outside of the house. Sakharam brings in an image of Ganpati, and he is followed by Dawood, who is playing the cymbals. Both are in high spirits. Sakharam does not believe in God, but now he brings an image of god in his house. When Laxmi entered his house for the first time, he was unconscious about the religion and its rites, but now he is celebrating the Ganpati in his house. That is the change is noticed in Sakharam for Laxmi. It is one of the most important scenes of this play where Vijay Tendulkar treats the communal problem of India in a frankly way. Dawood is Muslin, and he participates in the prayer with Sakharam, but Laxmi is a pious Hindu woman, and she avoids Muslims in religious prayer. She prevents Dawood to participate in the prayer but on the other hand, Dawood eagers to participate. At least Laxmi is beaten by Sakharam for preventing Dawood to participate in the prayer with him and tells Dawood to come regularly for the prayer.

Scene VII

Laxmi's moans are heard from the kitchen, and Sakharam rebukes Laxmi for her refusal of permitting Dawood to join the prayer for his Muslim background. He approaches God, looks for the aarti things, finds a matchstick and lights the aarti lamp, and he begins to sing the aarti in a dissonant voice. Sakharam tells Dawood to come tomorrow for aarti, and nobody will stop him from doing so.

Scene VIII

Sakharam is a possessive man, and as the master of the house, he thinks that Laxmi should act according to his wishes. She must laugh whenever she is asked to laugh by Sakharam. After the brutal beating, the whole body of Laxmi is throbbing with pain, and she is told to laugh; otherwise, Sakharam will go through her out from his house. She laughs, but it is punctuated with agonized moans, and on the other hand, Sakharam also does his intoxicated laugh and plays his mridanga.

Scene IX

The mridanga continues for some time. Sakharam beats the drum in a trance, and Laxmi comes in with the water-pots and carries them with a lot of effort to the kitchen. Sakharam shouts for tea and tells her to make it quickly. She is tired of pulling water's pots, and Sakharam orders her to make tea. He has no sympathy for her, and it seems that Laxmi is made to serve him. At least she bursts out on Sakharam, and she does not feel afraid of him. She has been living with him for one year, and she has not taken a rest for a single day, whether sick or fasting. She has been tortured every day and night across the year. She has received in this house nothing but work. In short, for Laxmi, Sakharam does not show any generosity, and she is the puppet for him. But Sakharam tells stories of his generosity that he has helped her when she has been driven out by her husband, and he has brought her and provides food, clothes, and shelter to her. He will perform her last rite after her death. These are done by Sakharam for Laxmi. Both are talking about suicide from the relief of boring life. But Laxmi stops doing it; she will not do that because it is unworthy of destroying her life through suicide as her mother carried her in her womb for nine whole months, and she can't kill herself in a breath. She belongs to a Brahmin family, and her father used to be a Musnif, and such an act decreases the reputation of her blood. Sakharam tells her that her father's reputation is unworthy for her as she has been thrown over from her husband's house. He also informs that she is the seventh woman in this house, and already six women lived with him. Laxmi tells Sakharam that he has done nothing favour to her, and he tells her to leave his house. Laxmi has no interest to live with Sakharam, as all know what happened here. She is bored with barking orders, curses, oaths, threatening to throw out, kicks, and blows. Laxmi informs Sakharam about her nephew, who lives in Amalner and intends to live with him whenever she likes to go. Sakharam attempts to throw her out, but she re-enters. Dawood comes to the house of Sakharaam when both Laxmi and Sakharam are quarrelling. They are taking chilum, and Laxmi goes on cocking in the kitchen.

Scene X

Sakharam beats the mridanga furiously, and a dim light is in both the rooms. Laxmi is lying on her rags in the kitchen. Voices from outside the house ask him to stop beating the mridanga. In this scene, Vijay Tendulkar shows some changes in the character of Sakharam. He has not been drinking so much this last year and does his puja regularly. Sakharam tells Laxmi to lead a liberal life, and she can go her own way as they are not married. In short, Sakharam is now going to free her from his possession. He makes free her, permits her to go to her nephew's house in Amalner. Sakharam wants to give a good farewell to Laxmi, and he will buy a ticket for her, give her a sari, a choli, and some money.

Scene XI

In this scene, Vijay Tendulkar describes the departure of Laxmi from the house of Sakharam for her nephew in Amalner. She lives here for a whole year. He assures Laxmi that he will feed her black ant in her absence.

Scene XII

After the departure of Laxmi, both friends Sakharam and Dawood are taking ganja. Sakharam shares his attachment for Laxmi, who is unique and has put a mark on him. It is the nature of Sakharam that he brings one woman after the departure of the present one. After Laxmi, he is talking about his new bird with Dawood, and very soon, he will bring her to this house. He has traced the wife of a police Fauzder in Chimkhada. The Fauzder will be left by his wife very soon, and as the wife has nobody besides a stepmother, it will easy for Sakharam to bring her into this house. Here Vijay Tendulkar has pointed out that Sakharam targets those women in society who have none, and he uses their wretched condition of life to enforce them to live with him.

Act II

Scene I

The Act II of the play contains the same setting. It opens in the house of Sakharam Binder, and it has two rooms, one outer and a kitchen. It opens in the evening after a few days later of Laxmi's departure from the house. Sakharam enters the house, carrying a leather bag, and he is followed by a woman named Champa. She is the new bird in the cage of Sakharam after Laxmi. Champa is the eighth numbered, and she is the wife of Fauzder, who is recently left by her. Here Sakharam gives a detailed account of the rules and customs of his house to the new bird. He introduces himself and his house to Champa as he has done with Laxmi. Sakharam tells her that it is the house of Sakharam Binder, not a king's palace. He is the master of this house, and it is he who can give orders, and nobody is allowed to give orders in this house. As a man, he is a hot temper and beats the life out of people when he loses his temper. He is foul-mouthed, and there is always a bidi or an oath on his lips. Sakharam gives her two saris in a year and two square meals per day. He also talks about the well, the water problem in summer, fetching water from the river, and the monsoon scorpion. Sakharam guides Champa on how she must conduct with the visitors to this house. Champa should not look up visitors to this house while she talks, and the stranger is not allowed to enter this house in his absence. In the mid of their conversation, Dawood comes to look at the new bird of Sakaharam, but he hurries away after a brief talk with Sakharam. Champa possesses a lusty figure, and Sakharam is infatuated with the body of Champa. Sakharam tells her to go to the kitchen to tea for her master and for her, but she, unlike Laxmi, does not go to the kitchen; instead, Champa tells him to go and find something to eat. Sakharam is shocked for Champa's conduct as in this house he gives orders to women whom he brought, but here Champa gives him orders rather than taking orders. Sakharam is confused with the changing atmosphere in his house. Champa is not a devoted woman like others for Sakharam. She says that she scares none. Sakharam comes to know about her husband, police Fauzder, who has been sacked from his job for a pistol stolen from the station. Champa never makes tea in all her life. Her mother-in-law used to make tea in her husband's house, and at her home, her old man used to make tea. Champa relates Sakharam with stories of her first encounter with her husband, Fauzder, and her marriage with him. Champa and her family had a good business and used to sell liquor. The police Fauzder came to raid the place, but he raided something else. He looked at her, fell in love, and kept saying to marry him. At least Champa has married him. Sakharam relates Champa with the story of Laxmi, who has just left the house. She was dutiful and carried all orders of Sakharam. Champa comes to know that Sakharam has bought a ticket for Laxmi, and he has given her a sari and a choli. In the mid of their conversation, Dawood comes once again, and Champa tells him to bring a nice pan with tobacco. Sakharam gives money to him to bring two pans. Dawood brings pans for them and also makes tea and serves it to Sakharam and Champa. Here Vijay Tendulkar narrates the violation of Sakharam's laws, and for the first time, a man enters the kitchen for tea. The difference between Act I and Act II is that in the first act, Sakharam controls the house and dominates his bird, but in the second act, the house is controlled by his bird and Sakharama is dominated by the lusty figure of his bird. Champa is bold in nature, and she begins to change her clothes at the presence of Sakharam and Dawood, that embraces them. In such a situation, Sakharam tells Dawood not to come to his house from now, and he will go to meet Dawood at his shop. Champa wants to sleep and asks Sakharam to wake her up when the food is cocked. Here Sakharam once again is shocked after tea. A woman makes food in the house, and Champa must make food, but she wants to sleep instead cocking food. Thus Champa once again violates the rule of the house. She thinks it is not a school, court, or something else where the rule is violated. She spreads out her rags on the floor of the kitchen, curls upon them, with her hands under her head, and within a few seconds, she is in asleep. Seeing such an incident in his house, he becomes restless now, shuts the front door, comes to where she is, and sits down. Suddenly unable to control himself, Sakharam lays his hand on her, and she sits up with a loud and weird shout. Sakharam, deeply mortified, hastily puts on his jacket and goes out. Champa sits alone drowsily, pulls out a small box from under the rags, takes some tobacco out, rubs it well on her palm, and stuffs it in her mouth.

Scene II

It is day, and the sunlight is streaming in. Sakharam is lying on his back on the mattress. The house door is open, and a stranger, dressed in khaki, comes to the door, wearing a police cape. It is the husband of Champa, Fauzder Shinde, and he is unshaven and looks dissipated. He pays an unwanted visit to the house of Sakharam to meet his wife, Champa. Like Sakharam, Fauzder Shinde is also attached to the lusty figure of Champa, and he can't forget her. Sakharam tells him to leave the house, but he sticks to the house. Dawood also comes to the house of Sakharam and looks at Fauzder Shinde. Champa enters the house. She has gone down to the river for a bath and becomes shocked by an unwanted visit of her husband. She asks Sakharam why he has allowed her husband to come in, and she becomes violent. She moves forward, jerks her husband up by the collar, slaps him violently, rains blows on him, and kicks him. Both Sakharam and Dawood are watching the scene, and they are dumb by the character of Champa. Finally, Champa drags her husband, Fauzder Shinde, to the door like a sack of potatoes and throws him out. Sakharam and Dawood come forward to rescue Fauzder Shinde from the clutches of Champa. Sakharam prevents her not hit, but she says that he has spoiled her life. Fouzder brought her from her mother even before becoming a woman and married her when she didn't even know what the marriage meant and tortured her day and night. He stuffed chilly powder into that god-awful place where it hurts most. It becomes clear that as a wife, Champa, was brutally tortured by her husband, Fauzder, and for this reason, she has left her husband. Dawood drags Fauzder from the house of Sakharam to save him from Champa. Sakharam is socked once again for this bird, and it is totally different from the others.

Scene III

It is night, and Champa sleeps on the floor in the kitchen, Sakharam comes in and is watching her, and he can't resist touching her, and she reacts immediately and sits up. Sakharam is infatuated with the lusty figure of Champa and wants to have physical relation with her, but she has no desire to have so. Sakharam becomes irritated with the denial of Champa as none of the previous women did such a thing with him because he is the master and everyone obeyed his orders. At least he irritates with Champa's conduct. He goes out of the kitchen, Champa remains sitting in the kitchen. Sakharam takes a bottle of wine down from the shelf and puts it in his mouth. After thinking for a while, she also comes to the outer room and drags Sakharam in by the wrist, and she joins in drinking with Sakharam. Both are abnormal and intoxicate and have physical relation.

Scene IV

The time is morning, and both Sakharam and Champa are sleeping in the kitchen. He wakes up at the knock on the door, and Sakharam opens the door and is asked for coming to the Press. Sakharam goes inside the house, puts on his shirt, jacket, cap, and chappals, and leaves the house. He carefully closes the house door, and Champa is still motionless and sleeping in the kitchen.

Scene V

The time is midday, Champa is sitting by the stove and eating; Sakharam comes in from outside, takes off his chappals, and hangs up his jacket and cap on the peg. He returns home from the Press after half-day work as he has failed to concentrate on work in the Press. He is deeply attached to Champa, and her lusty figure diverts him from work in the Press. He wants more fun from Champa, who is eating and shows her reluctance for fun. He enrages with Champa and orders her to obey him in this house; otherwise, he will thrash the life out of her. After a short pause, she agrees to have fun. She gets the bottle of wine, drinks it, and starts to play with Sakharam. In the mean-time, Dawood comes in and watches them. He stares at Champa, whose clothes are in disarray.

Scene VI

It is night, and the light from a street lamp finds its way into the room through the kitchen window. Everywhere else, it is pitch dark, and for a while, Champa's faint moan is heard and asks Sakharam to come and have fun. She laughs and moans.

Scene VII

It is the day, and both Sakharam and Dawood are in the home. Champa is not at home, and Sakharam looks different as his face bears the traces of his new life. It seems that Sakharam is very happy with Champa. Dawood tells his friend that he can't afford to sit at home without work. For Champa and his fun, Sakharam has not gone to work for that last week. In this regard, he may be kicked out of the Press. Dawood's suggestion does not affect Sakharam. He considers himself quite fit and strong to find another job if he is kicked out of the Press. He can carry loads or breaks stones for a living. Here Vijay Tendulkar shows the impact of sex on Sakharam's financial background. Besides this, Sakharam is bold enough, and he does not care about society and its opinions for him and his bird, Champa. Dawood talks about the changes in the family, and he reminds Laxmi and her management in this house before Champa. For Laxmi, there was discipline in the house, but this discipline has gone for the new bird, Champa. Sakharam informs Dawood that Laxmi is the past for him and Champa is his present. She is dead as soon as she has left the house. He talks about Champa and her fun with him. Dawood goes, and Sakharam is left alone.

Scene VIII

It is the day of Dassera, and from far away comes the sound of the shehnai and of drums. Champa is in the kitchen, and she is doing her chores, and somehow she tries to keep her balance as she has taken wine. Sakharam enters the outer room. He becomes shocked to see Champa is in an intoxicated mood. She has drunk on a holy day like Dassera, and even she has not taken her bath. On a holy day, the woman of the house should look all clean and tidy, but here Champa is not conscious about it. She is drunk. Sakharam closes the outer door, hangs up his jacket and shirt on the peg, and takes down his mridanga and dusts it. Champa loses her balance and clings to his neck. Sakharam tries to push her away, but she won't. At least he pushes her, and she crashes against something and falls down.

Scene IX

A dim light is in the kitchen where Chamap and Sakharam are sleeping. There are continuous knockings at the door and asking for Sakharam, but both Sakharam and Chapma are silent, and they are still sleeping in the kitchen. The knocking stops, and they are not answered for their calls.

Scene X

It is night, and the dogs are howling in the dark. Sakharam and Chapma are sleeping, and there are repeated knockings at the door. Sakharam wakes up and opens the door. He is shocked that it is Laxmi who is at his door this very night. He asks her for her nephew and for the reasons of her arrival in his house. Laxmi informs him of the saddest story of her life in the house of her nephew. She has been thrown out of the house by her nephew as his wife has charged her with stealing. They were going to hand her over to the police, and she has escaped here. Laxmi tells Sakharam that she will stay with him and die here. Sakharam tells her to go away as he has another bird as soon as she has left the house, and at present, there is no place for her in this house, but Laxmi is reluctant to go away. Sakharam is stupefied, Laxmi stands before him and cowering, and in the kitchen, Champa turns on her side and mutters drunkenly. Champa asks Sakharam to come and sleep, but Sakharam still can't believe Laxmi is at his door.

Act III

Scene I

It is morning, Champa comes into the outer room with a broom in her hand, and she begins to sweep the house. She opens the door, and Laxmi appears in the doorway. Champa takes Laxmi as a beggar and asks her to move to the next door, but Laxmi remains silent and standing in the doorway. Laxmi informs her that she is not a beggar and she used to live in this house with Sakharam. She stayed here for a year and twenty-one days. Laxmi also says that Sakharam brought her on the fourth day of the new moon, and she hadn't eaten for six days. She also tells her tragedy and wretched condition after her depurture from this house. She lived with her nephew in Amalner, from where she has escaped from the police. Now she has no place to go, and she comes to Sakharam for her shelter and safety. Champa tells her to meet Sakharam, but she is informed that Laxmi has already met him. Champa comes to know that she has come at night, waited outside, and had not slept in the yard for the rain. In the morning, Laxmi has noticed Sakharam go for the Press, and she didn't stop him as he was already late for the Press. Champa was drunk and in deep sleep, and she couldn't listen to the knocking of Laxmi at night. Laxmi is a religious and pious woman, and she is shocked to know that Champa has taken wine on the holy day of Dassera. Champa tells Laxmi that she has been living with Sakharam for a couple of months, and she has come after Laxmi left Sakharam. Champa asks her to stay with them as Laxmi nowhere to go. In the kitchen, Laxmi notices that there are no pictures of gods and wants to know about the prayers of Sakharam. When Sakharam lived with Laxmi, he was a religious man and used to participate in prayer, but now he is far away from gods as Champa does not believe in gods. Laxmi thinks that God controls everything, whereas Champa thinks that God does nothing to her. Both the ladies are taking tea, and Laxmi talks about her kitchen partner, the black ant, who lived in this kitchen and was the raja for Laxmi. They involve in deep conversation. Laxmi shares her experience as a wife, and she was driven out by her husband as she could not bear children for her husband. On the other hand, Champa says that she has left her husband instead for driven out. Her husband is impotent in nature, and he was a lot of bother for her. Both Champa and Laxmi are talking about the relation between husband and wife and Sakharam Binder. Sakharam provides Laxmi food and shelter, whereas he satisfies the sexual urge of Champa. It is decided that both ladies will live together in the house of Sakharam. Laxmi will look after the house, and Champa will look after Sakharam. Laxmi is happy with this proposal, and as the demand of her life is very little. She is satisfied with a bit of rice, some buttermilk, and two saris. Here Vijay Tendulkar clarifies that the house of Sakharam is the safest place for neglected women like Champa and Laxmi.

Sakharam enters the room, and he seems to be in a bad mood for certain reasons. He is dissatisfied with his service in the Press as the authority wants more work for the same pay from its workers. The working hours in the Press are increased, but the payment remains unchanged. Sakharam has lost his temper for his service in the Press, and now he becomes too violent after looking at Laxmi in his house, whom he has asked to leave his house. There is no place for Laxmi in this house, and she is dead for him and for this house. It is the rule of Sakharam's house; if one leaves it, then she is not allowed to return. Laxmi has left it, and now she is not allowed to return. This rule has been maintained by him for years. Sakharam rides Laxmi from his house, and she suddenly puts down the pail of water and the jar by the feet of Sakharam and falls at Sakharam and requests not to send her away as she has no place to go. He wants to free his feet from Laxmi but fails. At least he begins to rain blows on Laxmi, she doubles up in pain, but she will not let go of his feet. From a distance, Champa is watching the scene, and she comes ahead to rescue Laxmi from the blows of Sakharam. She takes Laxmi to the kitchen, and on the other hand, Sakharam repeatedly tells Laxmi to leave his house. Sakharam orders Champa to ride out Laxmi from his house as he is the master of it, but she denies it. She says that Laxmi will look after the house, and she will look after him. For this service, Laxmi will be received used and old saris of Champa. Here Champa very craftily manages Sakharam and creates an environment of Laxmi in this house. Sakharam begins to play his mridanga; Dawood enters the house and looks at Laxmi and Champa. He is silent after looking at Laxmi in this house once again.

Scene II

The night is far advanced, and a dim light is in the kitchen. In this scene, Vijay Tendulkar presents two contradictory pictures. One belongs to Laxmi, and another is Champa. Laxmi claps her hands softly in the kitchen and mutters the song 'Sitaram, Sitaram, Sitaram, Jai Sitaram.' But on the outer room, Champa is with Sakharam, and both are drunkards. Sakharam is irritated with the muttering of Laxmi and orders her to stop it, or he will kill her for it.

Scene III

This scene is most important that stresses the character of Champa. It is afternoon, and there is nobody in the house. Laxmi opens the door and enters the house. She is panting heavily, and she looks as if she has just gone through a terrible experience in her life. She goes to the kitchen and sits before the pictures of her gods. She is shocked as she has found Champa with that Muslim Dawood, and both have a relation. Sakharam is unaware of this relation. Laxmi prays for the harmony of Sakharam's family. Suddenly the door is knocked, and Fouzder Shinde comes to meet his wife, Champa. Laxmi opens the door and finds Fouzder, who is looking even more haggard and uncared. His feet are bare, and his face is scarred. He is searching for his wife, Champa, and asks Laxmi for Champa. Fouzder Shinde destroys his life for his wife. He takes wine excessively and leads an intoxicated life. He is weak and unable to eat. He asks for water. He destroys his body by taking wine, and he is always in drunk. The intention of his visit to the house of Sakharam is to be beaten by his wife, Champa. He wants to die by her hand as his life is lack intentions. He has no job as he has been sacked from it; his beloved wife has left him and has no home. Laxmi tells him to go before Champa comes and asks him to come when she is not around for food. Here Laxmi expresses her personal views on the character of Champa. She considers her as a sinner as she betrays her master, Sakharam. Champa walks out on her husband, lives with another, and carries on with a third. She has three men in her life, and such a woman is considered a sinner in society.

Scene IV

It is evening, Champa is in the kitchen, and Laxmi enters with pots of water balanced with her head and hip. Champa comes to know about her husband's visit in the absence of her in this house in the afternoon. She warns Laxmi to act according to her, and she should not double-cross her as she is allowed to stay here for her. Laxmi lives in this house because of Champa. Later, Laxmi sits before her gods and prays for her life. She makes complaints about Champa to gods. Laxmi says to the gods that Fouzder Shinde is her husband, and he wants her, but she lives with Sakharam. Champa finds another man for her, whereas her husband is still for her. For such a nature, Laxmi prays gods not to forgive her.

Scene V

It is night both Champa and Laxmi are in the kitchen. Sakharam is in the outer room. Laxmi does her prayer, and Champa is cutting vegetables for tomorrow. Sakharam asks Champa to come out of the room for sleep, but Champa is busy cutting vegetables and is reluctant with Sakharam's calls. She is still in the kitchen. Sakharam wants to have a physical relationship, but Champa denies it. Sakharam becomes angry with the Champa and enforces her to have it. He is violent and angry with Champa. Laxmi is on the other side watches them. Here Vijay Tendulkar explains the sexual harassment of a woman by her man. This scene presents the marital rape that is found in most cases in society.

Scene VI

It is still night, less dark Champa is lying in the outer room and is murmuring. Sakharam comes to the kitchen and tells Laxmi to leave this house at this very minute. She asks for permission to stay here till morning, but Sakharam tells her to do now. Before leaving the house, Laxmi informs Sakharam about the unfaithful nature of Champa. Sakharam comes to know that every afternoon Champa goes to Dawood when he is in the Press. Here Sakharam becomes violented to know the relation between Champa and his friend, Dawood. He can't bear such information about Champa and begins to beat Laxmi.

Scene VII

It is still night, and it is less dark now. Laxmi is sitting motionless. Sakharam, after hearing the unfaithful character of Champa, puts his hands around her neck, grunts, and squeezes harder. Her suffocated wail grows fainter, and Champa is murdered by Sakharam, who cries out for murder. Laxmi gets up quickly and limps towards them. She stands motionless, looks at Sakharam and then at the prostrate figure of Champa. Laxmi is a self-controlled woman, and in this critical situation, she first controls herself and then Sakharam. She consoles Sakharam that she will stay with him, look after him, and do everything what he likes. She suggests Sakharam to bury the dead body of Champa before the morning. She wants to hide the crime of Sakharam. She also assures Sakharam that nothing will have happened with him for this murder. Laxmi considered herself a virtuous and pious woman, and her holly deeds will save Sakharam from this crime. Laxmi wants to bury Champa in the kitchen before the morning. She digs with a shovel as Sakharam is motionless. One after another, blows fall, followed by Laxmi's grunts. Suddenly there is a knocking at the door. Sakharam looks lost, and his condition is pathetic. Laxmi stiffens, and she hears the sound. Champa's husband, Fouzder Shinde, has come to be beaten to death by his wife, Champa, but his wife already dies. The play concludes with Laxmi's digging for the grave of Champa, Fouzder Shinde's visit to meet his wife, Champa, and Sakharam's motionless after his murder of Champa.

Critical Appreciation

Setting and Structure

The play, *Sakharam Binder*, is divided into three acts, and every act is divided into several scenes. The scenes are not lengthy, and they are short in structure. In the first act, Vijay Tendulkar presents the relation between Sakharam and his bird, Laxmi. The second act contains the description of Sakharam and his relation with Champa. The last act is known for three, and here Tendulkar describes all his major three characters. The play takes its action in the house of Sakharam Binder. The house contains two rooms, an outer room and a kitchen. The house's possessions are mridanga, chilum, some pictures of gods, matrass, some utensils in the kitchen, and other domestic elements. It is a play on gender discrimination, and Vijay Tendulkar presents some examples to show how women are discriminated against both in families and in society for the patriarch society. The play deals with the lives of those who are driven out from their families, and in society, they are hunted by the hunters like Sakharam Binder. The play relates to the insecurity of women both in their families and in society. In these two places, they face the cruelty of life.

Title

The play has been named after its central male character, Sakharam Binder. He works in the Press. Sakharam is an unmarried Brahmin, but he always considers himself as a Mahar or scavenger. The play deals with his unmarried life and his interest in women. Sakharam is a hunter of women, and he always targets the poor, helpless, departed, and wretched women. He brings them to his house and provides food, shelter, and security. These women look after his house, and at the same time, they satisfy his sexual urge. Sakharam is a possessive man, and he is the master of his house. His birds or women should act according to his orders. He is short temper and always rebukes his women. In the play, Vijay Tendulkar talks about the sixth, seventh, and eighth women of Sakharam. It is the habit of Sakharam that he brings one woman after the departure of the previous one. The sixth woman of this house died of T. B. After her death, Sakharam brings Laxmi. After the departure of Laxmi, he brings Champa, the last woman in his house. Sakharam is the representative of the patriarch society where women have no place for existence. Throughout the play, Vijay Tendulkar shows the sexual exploitation of women in the world of Sakharam. Here Sakharam stands for all those men in the society who utilises their patriarch power over the women like Laxmi and Champa.

Security of Life

Vijay Tendulkar, in this play, highlights the insecurity of women. They face existential crises both in the family and in society. The women like Laxmi may be thrown out of the family at any time, and, for livelihood, they have to work under the men like Sakharam. Laxmi is driven out of her husband's house because she was unable to produce children. Thus there is no security for Laxmi in the house of her husband. Likewise, in the house of Sakharama, she faces insecurity. Both Champa and Laxmi can live with Sakharam till they act according to his orders. If they deny him, then there is no place for them. Laxmi has no children, and it brings insecurity for her in the house of her husband, she is also bored with Sakharam's order, and she escapes from Sakharam to the house of her nephew, but in the house of her nephew, she has also no security and escapes from there to Sakharam. Champa has no security in life. She has left her husband's house as he is impotent, but she faces an existential crisis in the house of Sakharam. She disobeys the rules of Sakharam's house and makes relation with

Sakharam's friend, Dawood. At the end of the play, she is murdered by Sakharam. As a man, Sakharam can have relations with several women, bringing one after another. Champa does the same, and like Sakharam, she also wants to satisfy her sexual urge and lives with Sakharam and makes relation with Dawood. There is no difference between Sakharam and Champa in this regard. But Champa has no security in society like Sakharam, and she has been murdered.

Religion and Sexuality

In this play, Vijay Tendulkar highlights two major themes throughout the story. These are sex and religion. It is sex that dominates all the relations in this play. Sakharam is a man of sex, and he brings women into his house for his sexual satisfaction. He brings Laxmi and then Champa for himself, not for looking after the house. Champa comes to live with Sakharam for food and shelter, and she has left her husband as he has failed to satisfy her. She is bold. She also makes relations with Dawood, Sakharam's Muslim friend. Champa does not believe in God, and she considers that God has done nothing for her. On a holy day of Dassera, she takes wine, whereas all Hindu women clean the house and pray for God. Laxmi is a pious and religious woman. She believes in gods, and she regularly prays for gods in the house of Sakharam. After the murder of Champa by Sakharam, she assures him that nothing will happen with Sakharam as she is with him, and her piousness will save him for this crime.

Characters

Laxmi

She is the seventh woman in the house of Sakharam. She is the daughter of a Munsif and has been thrown out by her husband as she has failed to have children for him. She is a pious and religious woman and has lived with Sakharam for one year. A big black ant is the companion of Laxmi in the house of Sakharam. She becomes bored with Sakharam and has left for the house of her nephew in Amalner. But she has returned to Sakharam from her nephew's house. Laxmi is a religious woman, and she does not like Dawood to participate in Ganesh aarti with Sakharam. She likes to fast, and prays before the gods. Laxmi is shocked to know about Champa and her drinking in the holy days like Dassera. Laxmi finds out the relation between Champa and Dawood. She tells about it to Sakharam. After the murder of Champa, Laxmi consoles Sakharam, manages to dig a grave in the kitchen to hide the body of Champa. Laxmi is a tolerated woman, and she has tolerated all the brutal conducts of Sakharam, and she also wants to help him at the end of the play.

Champa

Champa is the eighth woman in the house of Sakharam. She has married a police, Fouzder Shinde. She has left the house of her husband as he is impotent. She lives with Sakharam, but she violates the rules of his house. She does not always follow Sakharam's orders. Champa possesses a lusty figure that seduces her husband, Sakharam, and Dawood. She can satisfy the sexual urge of Sakharam, but she is not satisfied with him. To satisfy herself, she makes relation with Dawood. Champa allows Laxmi to live in the house of Sakharam for the second time. The play concludes with the murder of Champa, and she has been murdered by Sakharam as she has made relation with his Muslim friend, Dawood.

Dawood

Dawood is the Muslim friend of Sakharam. He is a regular visitor to the house of Sakharam. Both friends take ganja and talk about the women. Dawood is also a hunter of women. He is the friend of Sakharam, but he cheats his friend as he makes relation with his bird, Champa. Laxmi is a religious woman, and she prevents Dawood to participate in the Ganesh aarti in the house of Sakharam. Dawood has pointed out the changes in the house of Sakharam after the departure of Laxmi. He talks about how Champa has changed the atmosphere of the house.

Fouzder Shinde

He is the husband of Champa. He has met Champa for the first time during a raid in the area where Champa and her family sold wine. He is infatuated with the lusty figure of Champa and offered her marriage. They are married, but for Champa, he is impotent, and his wife has left him. He visits the house of Sakharam to meet his wife, where he is beaten by his wife, Champa. He keeps his visiting and wants to die at the hand of his wife, Champa. Fouzder has been sacked from his service as he is responsible for the loss of a pistol. At least he has no home, no wife, and no service. He is addicted to wine and drinks heavily.

4
Kanyadaan

Summary

Act One

Scene One

The play opens in the morning between ten and eleven in an old building block in a middle class colony. The action of the play is performed in the drawing-room of Nath Devlalikar. It is small but neatly arranged. The pictures of Mahatma Gandhi, Acharya Narendra Dev, Yusuf Meherali, and Sane Guruji are on the room walls. Nath Devlalikar is approaching sixty and seems to be active. Both Nath and his wife, Seva, are social reformers and activists. They have a daughter, Jyoti, and a son, Jayaprakash. Jyoti is twenty, and Jayaprakash is twenty-three years old. Nath is a Member of the State Legislative Council. He is an MLA and prepares for a journey. He makes a call to the controller of the bus service, asking for the bus from Pune to Asangaon. But Nath is not satisfied with the bus controller's conduct for his lacking information about the buses' schedules, and a controller should have all information about the schedule. Jyoti helps Nath with packing, and she watches him. She tells her father or Bhai that it is his special approach of his character to remind all the people in the world of their duties. Nath replies that both Jyoti and Jayaprakash are still young to understand the responsibilities and duties. Before India's independence, Nath had a vision of a future liberal India; he is now forced to see a different country, a different nation. He tells Jyoti to pack his shaving brush and the towel. He talks about discipline in life, and everyone must have it. The discipline is a matter of educating the mind, but the present time has stayed miles away from the disciplined society. Seva, the wife of Nath, is out of the home. She has gone to attend some social activities. Both Nath and Seva are busy with their social works, and most of the time, they are out of the home. They rarely stay home together for some time. Before leaving for the Asangaon, Nath interrogates Jyoti about the schedule of Seva's arrival. Jyoti informed Nath that Seva's rally would be ended by noon on the previous day, and she would be in this house by night or by eleven o'clock that day. Nath has to leave before the arrival of his wife. They have passed two weeks in this way. When his wife, Seva, goes to Bombay for a women's camp, Nath stays home to deliver lectures in Pune, and if she comes from Bombay to Pune, Nath has to go to Aurangabad to take part in a rally in favour of the people's rights. They play this hide-and-seek game. Jayaprakash, who is the only son of Nath, assures his father that he and his sister are at home to convey messages for their parents. Such a life of Seva's partnership is considered co-existence by Nath, and he wishes to review it seriously in the future. He wants to make a healthy relationship with his wife, Seva, as they cannot manage time for each other, and they fail to pass the time together with their son and daughter. Nath asks for packing his medicine bottles because he needs them as if the stomach is not in order and his speeches become worthless as nothing strikes his mind while delivering speeches for his stomach's problems. Jyoti wants to say something about her life to her parents, and Nath heartily welcomes her. He is a follower of democracy, and the spirit of democracy must be maintained in his house. Jyoti is above eighteen, and she has the right to present her own opinions, and Nath inspires her to express her opinions. Nath says that they have democracy in that house, and they are proud of it. His family does not know two-timing tricks that democracy is outside and dictatorship in the home. Jyoti wants to tell it for the last fifteen days, but she fails. She wants to tell when both Nath and Seva are home together. In the meantime, Seva comes home, and Jayaprakash brings the luggage of his mother. Seva thinks that her husband, Nath, has probably gone, but he is at home as the bus is late. Nath makes fun with Seva and says that he is not waiting for his wife because the call for the nation is far more important than the call of a wife. They narrate their past stories of marriage at Jyoti. There were two or three up-and-coming leaders in those days, and they had an interest in young Seva, and Nath was a third or fourth rank worker. But the strange thing was that Seva had chosen Nath rather than these upcoming leaders. Seva explains her reasons behind the selection of Nath. She considered that Nath was perfect and had a chance to be a minister or something. It was her dream to show off a bit if Nath were a minister. But the Janata party comes into power, and Nath stays an ordinary MLA. After a brief conversation on their marriage and political career, Nath informs Seva that their daughter, Jyoti, wants to say something to them, and they should listen to her. They are busy with their works and are not able to manage time for their children. After a journey, Seva is tired and wants to wash, but Nath enforces her to listen to first Jyoti and asks her to wash later.

Jyoti is over eighteen and informs her parents that she has decided to get married. This information surprises Seva, but Nath warmly greets her. She also informs that she is going to get married to Arun Athavale. He is a Dalit and doing his BA in Pune. He works part-time in 'Sramik Samachar'. Jyoti has met Arun in the Socialists' Study Group, where he has been coming for the past two months. Seva wants to be concerned with the family background of Arun and his parents, but Nath considers it is useless as his main concern about Arun. Nath is an activist for the development of Dalit society. He is a passionate and ideal leader and believes that his daughter's decision to marry Dalit results from his political philosophy. Nath is a lover of democracy, and he thinks that it is maintained both inside and outside of his family. He is too blind with his political ideology that he never considers other situations for marriage. Here Nath inspires his daughter to take a hasty decision in life. Nath has attended many inter-caste marriages, but now his family is going to celebrate such marriage. He wants to destroy the discrimination in society under the name of caste and its systems, and he wants to present his family as a prime example in this regard. Jyoti informs that the family of Arun lives in a village called Chiroli near Karhad, and they have a bit of land. There are seven children in the family, and Arun is the second one. His elder brother does nothing, and his father works in the field, but that is not enough to maintain his family, so he has to send money home every month. The other brothers of Arun go to school when it is possible. In short, the responsibility of the entire family falls on the shoulder of Arun. Such family background does not satisfy Seva, but Nath has no objection to his daughter's decision as he is a lover of democracy and prioritises Jyoti's decision, and he is blind with his political philosophy and ideology. Jyoti also points out the artistic qualities of Arun that he is a writer. Arun has written poetry and, at present, is writing an autobiography. She likes his poetry and has read some parts of his biography. Jyoti is pleased with his writing and wants to do anything to make Arun happy. Here one thing is clear that Arun, as a Dalit, has witnessed the discrimination and faced the brutality of society. Such harsh experience of life is expressed through his writings. The soft-hearted readers, like Jyoti, are impressed with his writings, and Arun is capable of grabbing the sympathy of such readers. Jyoti is emotionally attached to the misery of Arun's life, and she thinks to sacrifice her life to make Arun happy. All the above, Seva wants to know Arun is trustworthy or not. For a happy and healthy relationship between husband and wife, trust is essential. Here Seva is practical, and she is not blind like her husband. Like Nath, Seva is also a socialist, but she is practical. Jyoti is not sure about the trustworthiness of Arun as she personally does not know him much. She reads him and has come close to him. Jyoti feels that she can trust him, but she is not fully concerned with the trustworthy nature of Arun. But Nath thinks for a healthy relationship between husband and wife, the topic trustworthy is not important. He believes Jyoti loves a Dalit and wants to marry him; that is enough. Here both Seva and Nath possess different views of conjugal life. Seva thinks that trustworthiness is essential for a healthy marital life, whereas Nath denies its priority and considers love is essential for healthy relation.

Vijay Tendulkar here presents the blind love of a father towards his daughter pushes her to take a hasty and wrong decision. It becomes clear to Seva that her daughter, Jyoti, will make a hasty decision to marry Arun. Jyoti knows nothing about Arun, and she is just infatuated with his writing and has decided to marry him. Seva knows how to select the right partner as a woman in life. She has selected Nath after a keen observation on him and his character for a long time, but here her daughter does the opposite and does not ready to spend time on observation to Arun. It is right for a woman to wait for two or even three or four years to gather information about a man should study the information in-depth and think about marrying him. But here, Jyoti does nothing; she has felt in love with Arun for his poetry and writing. Like Jyoti, Nath is also hasty to make a decision about Arun. He takes Jyoti's side and suggests that Jyoti will assist Arun in the financial field to manage the family as Jyoti will not be a homebound housewife. All problems of Arun will be tackled by Jyoti as she is capable of doing it. At least Nath agrees with Jyoti and her choice of Arun, but Seva considers it as hasty. Jyoti wants to invite Arun to meet with her parents. Seva is a fighter for the abolishment of the untouchable system in society. She is very familiar with the untouchable culture and the Dalit culture. On the other hand, Jyoti's life belongs to a certain manner and has been brought up in a specific culture. She tells Jyoti that it is not easy for her to manage life in the Dalit society that is adverse from her present situation. Besides it, Jyoti has no chance to come back after the marriage to mend life's mistakes. So here, Seva suggests her to take a decision after very careful observation. Seva, in short, attempts to teach her to utilise her democratic power rather than to misuse it. Nath is ready for his journey, and he also comes to know that Seva is staying home for the whole week. He also informs that he will return by the evening. Seva also wants to know from Jyoti about the closeness of her relationship with Arun, and she gets relief after knowing it. Seva wants to change her clothes as she has been sitting in the drawing-room since she has come. Then the phone rings, and Seva receives the call. It is a call from Kusum, who informs that the women have no work on hand and they have completed the Godrej order. Seva, over the phone, suggests Kusum call the manager of Mehta Company for the work of women.

Scene Two

The scene opens in the same place, the same drawing-room in the evening. Jyoti opens the door with a latchkey, and she enters the room. She is followed by Arun Athavale. He is probably about twenty-four or twenty-five years old and possesses a complexion dark and a stern face, yet he is good looking. There is nobody in the house except Jyoti and Arun. He has come to meet with Nath, Seva, and Jayaprakash. Jyoti informs Arun that her brother is doing MSc and he will return around five o'clock. Jyoti informs Arun that her mother, Seva, will return home around five-thirty and her father Nath was going to be at home, perhaps he had to go out somewhere, but he may return by six-thirty. Jyoti wants to make tea for Arun, but he asks to sit with him rather than make tea. Arun feels uncomfortable in this house which seems to be a big one, as he generally lives in a small house. There are ten people live together in a room of eight feet by ten feet. The heat of their bodies warms them in winter. There are no clothes on their backs, no food in their stomachs, but in this small room, they feel safe. But the houses in the city seem to be like the bellies of sharks and crocodiles for Arun. Arun's psychological problem is to adjust himself in the city, and he fears the big houses. Such a problem is noticed when Jyoti is going to make tea for Arun, who has to stay alone in the drawing-room, and this room seems to a big belly that can eat him. So he stops Jyoti from making tea. It is a trauma of Arun in the city. He shares with her an incident that has happened with him in the previous night in the hostel. He was in the hostel with a fellow student, Nikhil, who was explaining dialectic materialism before sleep. Nikhil was sleeping, but Arun stayed awake. In this situation, it seemed that the building swallowed him up in a blink of an eye. Arun has been living in the city for quite some time, and yet he has failed to adjust to the city. It is strange for Jyoti after coming to know about such a problem of Arun in the city. She thinks that some people are scared of thieves, some of bandits, and ghosts. But the strange thing is for her that Arun scares big houses. Arun feels safe in the streets and in crowds, but his heart shudders when walls of cement and concrete surround him, and in this situation, he feels that he must get up, runs, and gets lost in the crowd. Jyoti asks Arun to follow her into the kitchen, but he neither allows Jyoti to go kitchen nor follows her. Their conversation is continued in the drawing-room. Arun tells Jyoti about the lives of his preceding generations. He talks about the lifestyle of his grandfather and great grandfather. Here Arun is a scavenger, and he shares the exploitation history of the scavenger generation after generation by the hand of the elite and high-class people in the society. Their grandfather and great grandfather used to roam barefooted miles after miles in the heat, in the rain through day and night. They also used to wonder, shouting 'Johaar, Maayi-bapp! Sir-Madam, sweeper!'. Here Arun attempts to introduce Jyoti to the harsh reality of Dalit life and culture. Generation after generation, their stomachs used to the stake, they have begged stinking bread, their tongues are always tasting the flesh of dead animals with relish. Arun lives with poverty as he belongs to Dalit society, and Arun can't afford ghee spread, wheat bread culture offered by Jyoti. Arun makes it clear to Jyoti what kind of life she would live after the marriage with Arun. She will have to eat stinking bread with spoilt dal and will shit every day in their slum's village toilet like his mother. At the same time, Jyoti will beg for a little grass for their buffaloes. Before the marriage with Jyoti, Arun clarifies that his life is not a socialist service camp where one comes and does services. The harsh reality of Arun's life shakes Jyoti, and she begins to weep. She cries for Arun and his reality, for her future with Arun. Jayaprakash opens the door with a latchkey, and he is embraced by seeing them and the crying face of Jyoti. Jyoti introduces Jayaprakash with Arun, and Jayaprakash goes inside. He realises that his sister is crying. In the drawing-room, they are alone, and Arun suddenly grabs her arm and twists it. Jyoti moans in pain; in the meantime, Seva enters the drawing-room, and she notices them. For her, it seems that Arun hits Jyoti as a punishment. Jyoti introduces her mother to Arun, who greets her, but Seva is not impressed or pleased by Arun. She asks Jyoti about the arrival time of Nath, who will probably arrive by five-thirty. Seva tells her daughter to make tea, and Jyoti goes inside for tea. Here Seva begins her conversation and attempts to know Arun very closely. She asks Arun about his future after completing education and his management of the household with Jyoti. But she is not satisfied with Arun's replies, but she becomes rather shocked. Arun does his BA, but he has not yet decided about his further education; he also does not plan to manage his household with Jyoti. In the present time, it is very difficult to obtain a flat in a city like Pune, and one must have fifty or sixty thousand rupees; otherwise, one suffers, and the wife has to suffer for no reason. Seva knows the complexity of management in the cities, and she wants to be assured of a comfortable life for her daughter Jyoti in Pune with Arun. But she is shocked after noticing a lack of seriousness in Arun for his domestic life. Arun has neither planned for civilised life nor he is serious about it. He is of descent, and he wants to lead his household with Jyoti like his ancestors. He informs that their financial problems will be solved by their family business of brewing illicit liquor. It is their family business, and it is an easy business; only one must know the technique. According to Arun, it is a first-class profession for two persons, the man bribes the police, and the wife serves customers, and the people call her aunty. Arun also informs that there are also services for children in this highly profitable business. The children wash glasses and plates, and they fetch paan and cigarettes for the customers. Arun talks about it with Seva and Jayaprakash, and they are speechless after hearing Arun. They are shocked to know the future of Jyoti, who will live with the owner of an illicit liquor shop and serve the drunkard people. Jyoti attempts to control the situation, and she tells Seva and Jayaprakash that Arun does fun sometimes, but on the other hand, Arun is very serious, and both Seva and Jayaprakash can feel it. But they are helpless at the decision of Jyoti to select Arun as her husband. Both Seva and Jayapraksh are tensed for this match. In the meantime, Nath enters the drawing-room, and he is very much pleased for the meeting with Arun. Like Jyoti, Nath is also unconscious of reality, and he also pushes Jyoti towards the dark side of her life. Nath is happy that his daughter will marry an inter-caste Arun as he is an activist to solve the caste problem in society. Nath is blind for his political philosophy that is far away from reality. As a socialist, he has attended many inter-caste marriages, but now it is the time for him to perform such marriage, and he considers that his home has become India in the real sense for selecting a Dalit as his son-in-law for his daughter, Jyoti. Like Jyoti, Nath is also a fan of Arun's poetry and asks him to recite some poems. Arun feels irritated and becomes uncomfortable. He suddenly gets up and says that he wants to leave. He walks determinedly towards the door and leaves the house without a backward look. Such abrupt departure of Arun shocks everyone in the drawing-room. Both Seva and Jayaprakash are not satisfied with this match, but Nath is happy with Arun; he possesses a liberal spirit and supports his daughter's decision. He maintains his fighting for liberty both inside and outside of his house. In his family, Seva and Jayaprakash prevent Jyoti nad her liberal decision, whereas Nath supports Jyoti and her liberty. He does not want to be a dictator father for Jyoti. Seva and Jayaprakash present their arguments for the denial of Arun as they have noticed that the culture of Arun does not fit with them, and it will spoil their daughter's life. Jyoti is a city girl and has been brought up around the civilised culture, whereas Arun is a Dalit and the Dalit culture, and its lifestyle is totally different from the civilised society. In such a situation, it is never possible for Jyoti to adjust to the Dalit society. But Nath denies this argument for the cultural background behind the denial of Jyoti's wedding with Arun. Seva also informs that Arun has planned nothing about their future life; he has not yet decided to lead a civilised lifestyle, rather than Arun has decided to lead the business of brewing illicit liquor. Nath is not serious about this information and takes it that Arun has made jock with them. Both Seva and Jayaprakash tell Nath that they have witnessed the rude conduct of Arun with Jyoti on this very day in this house when they have entered the house. They have caught her crying and blowing her right elbow when they have entered the house. Nath suggests them to ignore these, and he says that Arun is not a middle-class man and he is a Dalit, and he has been brought up amid poverty and hatred. Such background has probably impacted the psychology of Arun, and through his behaviours, sometimes it is reflected, so these should be ignored by the civilised people life Nath and his family. After the argument over Jyoti's match with Arun, Seva clarifies that she will never accept Arun as a son-in-law. As a socialist and activist, Nath encourages his wife to accept this marriage. He says that society can't be transformed through words alone. As socialists, they have to act as catalysts in this transformation. Nath extracts examples from history to mend the society. He says that the old socialists and reformers did not stop making speeches and writings articles on widow remarriages; many of them actually married widows, and thus, the society has been changed. Here both Nath and Seva are activists, and they are fighting for the Dalit people and their rights in society. Nath suggests that they should not stop giving lectures and writing articles for the Dalit people; they should do something in reality. Nath makes it clear that they should accept Jyoti's decision for Arun to transform society. In short, he wants to use as an experiment his daughter for his socialist career or to transform society. Nath and Seva are activists for inter-caste marriages, and it is time for them to do something real. But Seva does not like her husband's proposal and denies using her daughter, Jyoti, as an experiment in this field, whereas Nath wants to do it. Nath wants to know the decision of his daughter.

Jyoti informs her family that she does not know much about Arun; she knows little of him through his poetry and writing. She feels that she can trust him, but the very next moment, she is left miles away from him. For Jyoti, Arun is not bad at heart, and by nature, he is not vile. Human beings are complex, and Arun is also complex. She assures that she must understand the complexity of Arun, and once she understands his complexity, she can dispel that complexity. It is the nature of Jyoti that she can't run away after her commitment, and she has committed that she would marry Arun. Seva asks her to change her decision as she has committed it in a weak moment. But Jyoti affirms that she can't, and she will marry without Seva and Jayaprakash, whereas Nath approves of her. Nath clarifies that in democratic matters, discussions and controversies are common, but the decision of individuals must be sustained. His family is democratic, here the debate is noticed for Arun, but the final decision must be taken by Jyoti. Here Nath recites the discriminated history of the Dalit people. For generations, these people are tortured and betrayed by the people of Brahmin society and the elite class. Now it is a proud time for Nath and his family that their daughter breaks this system. She tries to cover the crimes of her ancestors who once dominated the ancestors of Arun. Here Nath fully supports his daughter and her decision to marry Arun.

Act Two

Scene One

It opens in the same drawing-room after some months. Within these months, Jyoti has married Arun, but her conjugal life is not satisfactory. She is dissatisfied with Arun. Her conduct for Seva, Jayaprakash, and Nath has changed. She avoids them. Jyoti returns from her work, and she is tired and crushed. She appears thinner and as if she has suddenly become older. Seva notices the strange behaviour of Jyoti after her marriage to Arun. She was absent from the house in the previous night and passed it in Dinanath's room. She did not make a call to inform Seva or Nath of her stay in Dinanath's room. Jyoti shows the excuse that she was caught up in office work for the whole day and didn't get time to inform Seva. The negligence of Jyoti for her mother torments Seva, and she thinks that Jyoti torments her as she has not allowed her to marry Arun and She takes revenge on her mother. But her strange behaviour is also tormenting her father, Nath, who has not made any mistake because he allowed her to marry Arun. He is unable to sleep, keeps awake late into the night worrying about her. Seva asks Jyoti to show a little consideration for her father, Nath, at least. Jyoti assures that such things will not be done again, but such assurance is not valid for Seva as Jyoti has done it several times. Seva attempts to make her conscious about the change in her character and in the atmosphere of this house. Jyoti is not open and frank as she was in this house before her marriage. She lives here like a stranger, takes shelter in this house out of sheer necessity. Here Nath did the most precious service, 'Kanyadaan' in his life, but this service has proved to be wrong in his life. So he is unable to concentrate on anything, and he broods day and night. Jayaprakash is present in the drawing-room, and he hears his mother. He tells Seva not to worry about Jyoti. He also can't understand why Bhai, his father, continues to be distressed as he had not only approved this match, but he had also actively promoted it, and at the wedding, he also danced. Seva tells Jayaprakash will understand the situation of his parents when he will be a father of a daughter and do 'kanyadaan'. Here Jayaprakash shares his philosophy of life with Seva. He says one should change according to the changes in the circumstances. Both Seva and Nath should change as the circumstances of the family have changed. But Seva informs that she and Nath have been taught by guruji not to adjust to the circumstances; they have been taught to change it according to them rather than adjust with it. In this way, Jayaprakash consoles his mother to recover from the grief for Jyoti. The doorbell rings, and it is Nath who enters the drawing-room. Nath talks about his rush journey from Bombay, but Seva suggests him to stay there to have an undisturbed sleep as he hardly slept last night, got up early in the morning and caught the Deccan Queen. Nath asks for a piping hot tea from Jayaprakash, and he feels relax to know of Jyoti's arrival. Both Seva and Nath were worried in the night as they did not have information about Jyoti. Seva thinks that Arun did not allow Jyoti to inform them as they did not allow their marriage. Once again, Nath takes his daughter's side and says that Jyoti was legal and had her free will to get married. Here again, both Seva and Nath are debating on the liberty of daughters to select life partners. Seva argues that it is not a rightful duty of parents not to prevent their daughters if they fall into a pit. In this regard, they should stop their daughters. It was their duty to stop Jyoti to select Arun, and Seva did so. But Nath supported Jyoti to fall into a pit. Nath also says that he would try his daughter to change her mind as a father, but he would not stop her as she insisted on jumping into that pit. Nath also argues that if Jyoti has married someone who is not a Dalit or any other fellow instead of Arun, there is no guarantee for peaceful nights. As they are the parents of a daughter, they have lost their rest at night. Every new relationship brings problems in its wake, and such problems are coming up with the new relation between Jyoti and Arun. In the mid of their conversation, Jyoti serves tea to Nath, suddenly Nath notices a mark on the shoulder of Jyoti. The mark shows that Jyoti has been beaten by Arun. Nath asks Jyoti about the mark, but Jyoti cannot say something; her eyes are filled with tears, her throat blocked, and she tries to suppress her tumultuous feelings; she gets up and rushes in to escape from her father. This mark also hurts Nath, and he decides that his daughter and son-in-law must live in his house so that he can look after his daughter and Jyoti may live with him. Seva does not like this proposal, and she also says nothing about it to Nath. At least Jyoti denies her father's proposal to stay with her father. She does not show any reason behind her rejection of her father's proposal. Jyoti clarifies that Arun will never enter this house as she has left him and she is not going back to him again. This information of Jyoti stuns everyone in the drawing-room. Here the earlier passion of Jyoti for Arun has been shattered with the harsh reality. She does not like to cry once again, and it was she who made this decision. The phone rings, and it is a call by Arun for Jyoti, but she receives the call reluctantly. Nath wants to save the relation of Jyoti and suggests his wife do so. In the meantime, Arun enters the house; he is drunk and calling for his wife, Jyoti. He has come to ask apology from Jyoti, whom he has been beaten badly. Suddenly he takes a knife out of his trousers' pocket to cut off his hands as a penalty. Jayaprakash snatches the knife from him. He informs Seva that he gets a little drunk, and Jyoti says something; he also says something; thus, the fight begins between them. Here Arun had beaten his wife when he was drunk. Arun tells his childhood story. As a child, he used to see that his father beat his mother regularly, and this domestic violence has impacted his life. Arun, as a scavenger, does not know the non-violence ways of Brahmin like Nath. They drink and beat their wives. They love their wives, but the beating gets publicised. Arun thinks of himself as a barbarian, drunkard, and wife-beater. Arun says that Jyoti has thought about his improvement after the marriage, but she is stupid because he has not changed after the marriage. At least Jyoti accepts the confession of Arun and ready to leave with Arum. Nath feels proud that his daughter does her duty as a perfect wife to mend her husband's character.

Scene Two

The scene opens after few months in the drawing-room of Natht's house. Nath is immersed in a book, and Seva enters, opening the door with a latchkey. He is highly pleased with the book. It is an autobiographical book of Arun. Nath has read such a fabulous book after many years. The quality of the language of Arun's biography is a true and it has a living language. It is utterly free from the impact of English. The book belongs one hundred per cent to their own soil. Nath is overjoyed by this book. On the other hand, Jyoti is pregnant by six months, and she has been admitted to Dr Khare's nursing home to avoid complications later as the bleeding has started again. There is an internal wound in her stomach. Seva returns home after admitting her daughter. Seva informs Nath that the neighbours of Arun suggest that Jyoti should not be allowed to stay with Arun as he beats her and even kicks her. Nath can't understand how Arun can do it. It is difficult for Nath to understand the character of Arun, who has written a beautiful autobiography where he describes the humiliation with extraordinary sensitivity, and he possesses himself a heinous character. He kicks his pregnant wife on her belly. Seva thinks that the Dalit can't understand what gratitude means as Arun does not want to work, and he remains a burden on Jyoti. Obviously, he will never feel grateful for her support, and he beats his pregnant wife. Seva also says that their Dalit son-in-law, who can write a wonderful autobiography and many lovely poems, actually wants to remain as an idler. He wants his wife to work, and with her money, he wants to drown himself in a drink. Seva also thinks that Arun kicks Jyoti as she belongs to the high caste, and in this way, he consoles himself and takes revenge for the injustice of his ancestors who were also kicked by the high caste once. This is Arun's time to avenge the high caste people for their torture of Dalit people in the past, and Jyoti is an instrument for his mental satisfaction. Nath is depressed with Jyoti's critical condition, and he thinks that if Jyoti dies in this critical condition, they will lose their only daughter, but on the other hand, Arun will lose nothing as he will get another wife. Seva wants to bring her daughter to this house alone to stay here at least for her delivery, but Jyoti does not agree with it. Jyoti will return to her filthy room in the slum this evening from the nursing home. Jyoti returns to the house of his husband rather than to the house of her father. In the mid of their conversation, the phone rings, and it is a call for Nath to attend a public discussion in favour of the autobiography of Arun, who has just become a renounced author in the society for the success of his autobiography. But Nath denies this offer to speak on the book of Arun. Nath is an MLA and father-in-law of Arun, and, naturally, he is the preferred figure in the public meetings in favour of Arun's biography. Seva expresses her desire to insult Arun in public if she is asked to speak. She will speak whatever the author has said about injustice and exploitation is the hypocrisy of the first order because of the author, Arun, himself does such things with her daughter or his wife, Jyoti. She will also inform that Arun lives on her daughter's blood, and on top, he gets drunk and bashes her up. Seva will speak that her daughter is exploited for her family background as she belongs to the high caste. In the mid of the conversation between Seva and Nath, Seva speaks about the points of view of Arun for them. Arun says that Seva is a procuress who supplies girls from the 'Seva dal' to the socialist leaders. He also says that Nath is not the father of Jyoti; it is guruji who is the father of Jyoti. Jayaprakash enters with an evening newspaper where the international news is printed. Here Vijay Tendulkar has pointed out the Middle-East conflict. He has cited the war between Israel and Palatines. During the Second World War, the Jews were butchered and killed by Hitler, and after the World War, the remaining Jews have founded their own country, Israel. Now the Jews are killing and dominating Palestinians. Here Jayaprakash says that once the Jews were dominated and tortured, and at present, they are dominating and torturing, those who were being massacred are now indulging massacres. Here Jayaprakash also suggests that Arun, as Dalit, tortures Jyoti now because the Dalit people were tortured by the high caste. It is the narrative technique of Vijay Tendulkar that he has used an international simile to explain the relation between Dalit society and the high caste. Seva, Nath, and Jayaprakash involve discussing the relation between Jyoti and Arun.

The doorbell rings, and it is Arun who enters the house, followed by two persons. One belongs to Arun's Dalit community, and the other is an upper-caste well-wisher of the Dalit community. Arun informs that he has not intended to come, but these two gentlemen drag him to this house. He introduces his companions to Nath and his family. He introduces his Dalit friend, Hammeer Rao Kamle, who is a noted essayist of Dalit literature. He is an excellent but neglected writer. The other man is Vamanseth Nevrgaonkar, a critic of Dalit literature and spends his money feeding Dalit writers. They have an association, 'The Progressive Dalit Literature Circle'. Arun becomes arrogant for the success of his autobiography and does not know how to talk with elders, especially Nath. He thinks the celebrated writer as the next in demand to the pet dog. He becomes proud for the success of his book and appreciates himself highly, and thinks that his book will get the Sahitya Akademic Award as he has done a big thing for Maratha Literature. Vamanseth Nevrgaonkar published Arun's autobiography, and a public meeting has been arranged in favour of this book. Nath has been selected for a chair in this meeting and will deliver a speech without his consent. His name has been printed on the posters and invitations. Here Nath has been emotionally blackmailed by Arun. If Nath fails to attend the programme, the people will say that father-in-law and son-in-law do not see eye to eye as Arun regularly tortures his daughter. After inviting Nath for the programme, Arun leaves with his two companions. He torments Nath and plays with his emotion. Nath's love for Arun has changed with hatred. He rebukes Arun for printing his name without his permission. Nath thinks Arun's very presence in his house has polluted the atmosphere, and he wants to clean it. Nath is a fighter and has fought many battles in an adverse situation. Generally, it seems that Nath is softer than wax, but his strength of conviction can shatter rocks to fragments. He denies participating in the programme. Seva suggests him to attend and deliver a speech because his refusal will bring more suffering for Jyoti as it makes Arun find a new way to torment her. For the sake of his daughter's safety and for Seva's argument, Nath is ready to attend the programme to deliver a speech in favour of the book.

Scene Three

The scene opens after the programme in the drawing-room of Nath's house. The time is nine o'clock. The door is opened with a latchkey, and Nath enters, followed by his wife, Seva, who switches on the light in the drawing-room. Nath sits down on the sofa, and he is dispirited, weary, tired, and listless. Jayaprakash enters the drawing-room from outside. He watches both his parents are depressed and tensed for their daughter, Jyot. Both Seva and Jayaprakash want to make Nath light from tension, and they attempt to please him. Jayaprakash wants to serve water, coffee, and play music for Ravi Shankar, but Nath does not interest Jayaprakash. He tells Nath that the speech was the most balanced, measured, and to the point. He has delivered a perfect speech on the book of Arun. But for Nath, the speech was rubbish, hollow, hypocritical, flat, and meaningless drivel. When Nath had read the book, he praised it, but after coming to know the actual character of Arun, he begins to neglect Arun and his book. He feels that the book has no ounce of truth in it; it is a hoax. The book is nothing but a crafty, sanctimonious, and artistic hoax. For Nath, the book is not an autobiography; it is pulp fiction based on half-truths. But in the programme, Nath has delivered a good speech in praise of the book, presents a lying speech. His blatant lying today will make Jyoti's life a little more tolerable. Now Nath repents for his mistake for the approval of Jyoti's marriage with Arun. He tells Seva that she warned him several times, but he did not pay any attention to her. He was blind and had the maniacal urge to uproot the caste system and caste distinctions from society, and he pushed his daughter into the sea of misery. After attending the programme, Nath is under severe strain, and he is asked for rest, but he resists it. He is totally broken and goes inside for rest. The doorbell rings, and it is Jyoti who has come to meet her father, Nath. She wants to talk only to Nath. She wants to leave the house when she comes to know that Nath is inside for sleep. But Nath comes in the drawing-room; he sees Jyoti and walks forward to her with great affection. Both are also talking about the delivered speech of Nath. He says that he has presented a lousy speech which is a bad, wretched, and shameful performance. But Jyoti repeatedly asks her father behind the reasons for his coming to the meeting to deliver a speech in favouring the book. Nath says that he was invited, and his name was printed in the posters and invitations, but Jyoti denies such arguments presented by Nath. She assures Nath that he has come to the meeting in fear of Arun that Arun would torture her more if he did not. He attended the programme to save his daughter from the torture of Arun. Nath went there against his wishes and praised that book against his wishes. Jyoti tells her father not to do it for her as she belongs to Arun. Nathe should not show any mercy for her as she belongs to someone. Nath is an idealist figure, and he says that he does not hate Arun, but he hates his tendencies. No man is fundamentally evil, he is good, and he contains propensities towards evil and must be transformed. But Jyoti tells that such idealism of life of her father, Nath, influenced her from childhood. She presents an explanation of Arun's character. He is a savage beast, an idiot, a demon, and also a poet. Jyoti clarifies that she accepts Arun, whatever he is, and she can't reject him. Through their conversation, Nath asks Jyoti to leave Arun, but she denies it. She considers it as a battle for her to live with Arun, and she has never been taught to leave a battleground. She has never been learned to bow down in any adverse circumstances. She can't return as she is a soldier and is taught by her father to fight in an adverse situation. So she decides to live with Arun until the end of her life. Here Jyoti has been pissed up between her father's ideology to live like a soldier and the reality of life. At least Jyoti accepts to live in her world with Arun, where she wants to die. Jyoti is pregnant and tells her parents not to worry about her delivery. She will not come to this house as she has her husband to look after. She is not Jyoti Yadunath Devlalikar now; she is Jyoti Arun Athavale. At the end of the play, Jyoti leaves the house of her father, and Nath looks in the direction of Jyoti's exist. He breaks down, buries himself in the sofa, and shrinks into it.

Critical Appreciation

Title

The term "Kanyadaan" in the title has its specific meaning in Indian culture. It is considered as greatest and risky daan for the parents in their lives. According to the Hindu ritual in the weddings, a father has to give his daughter to his son-in-law, and after the wedding, the daughter leaves the house of her father permanently. She comes after the wedding to her father's house as a guest. A father always thinks about his daughter, who he has nourished and brought up. He passes restless nights for his daughter after the wedding. In this play, Vijay Tendulkar presents the plight of a father after his Kanyadaan. Nath is the father of Jyoti, and he has given the hands of his daughter to Arun. Before the wedding, he was excited, but all his excitement has been shattered after the wedding. Nath has given the hands of his daughter to the wrong person who spoils his daughter's life and takes the peace and harmony from his life. Nath and his family lead a harmonious life, but the harmony of his life has lost after his kanyadaan. Here Vijay Tendulkar has used an appropriate title for his play.

The play's action takes place in the drawing-room of Nath, and the building is in a middle-class colony. There are pictures of Mahatma Gandhi, Acharya Narendra Dev, Yusuf Meherali, and Sane Guruji on the room walls. Here Vijay Tendulkar presents the relation between high caste Hindu society and Dalit society. In the history of Indian class struggle, it is noticed that the subaltern, Dalit, and untouchable people have been dominated for generations by the elite high caste Hindu society; in this play, Vijay Tendulkar presents a different picture. Nath belongs to a high caste and is an activist for Dalit society; he has married his daughter to a Dalit. But in this play, it is noticed that the Dalit and subaltern people are not dominated; rather than they dominate the high-class people. Arun is a Dalit, and he torments Nath, his daughter, Seva, and Jayaprakash.

Marriage and Marital Life

The marriage, conjugal life, and selection of husband for a lady are the most important points highlighted in this play. Vijay Tendulkar has mentioned two marriages, the first one is between Nath and Seva, and the second one is between Jyoti and Arun. The first marriage is successful, and Seva has selected a perfect life partner, whereas the second is a failure, and Jyoti has failed to select a perfect partner. Before selecting Nath as a husband, Seva has taken enough time to observe his character, and after careful observation, she has selected Nath as her husband. But in the case of Jyoti, the incident is different. She has no patience like her mother, Seva, for selecting a husband. She takes a hasty decision. She has met Arun and within two months has decided to marry him. In both cases, the bridegrooms have selected their life partners. Jyoti's hasty decision for Arun later spoils her life where Seva's timely decision proves to be correct. The next important difference between these two marriages is the backgrounds of the couples. Seva has selected Nath, who is like herself, a socialist and activist. They have the same interest in life, and they belong to the same class. So there is not any difficult for them to adjust with each other. But in the case of Jyoti, the situation is different. Jyoti belongs to a high caste society and has been brought up under a cultural atmosphere; on the other hand, Arun belongs to a subaltern society, and he is far away from the civilised culture, and he is habitual with a barbarian life. It is naturally difficult for Jyoti to adjust with Arun in the Dalit subaltern society after her marriage. Here Vijay Tendulkar gives a message for his readers on the serious subject to select life partners. He finds that the decision-making system and backgrounds of the couples are most important for a healthy relation.

Idealism Vs Realism

It is a play where Vijay Tendulkar shows how the great idealism of life has been defeated at realism. Nath possesses an ideal view of life and society, and he thinks that all people are good; he loves them but hates their bad tendencies. He is an activist of Dalit society and has attended many inter-caste marriages. He is blind with his idealistic views of life, and he accepts the proposal of his daughter, Jyoti, to marry a Dalit. His wife, Seva, is also a socialist, but she is realistic about Jyoti's proposal to marry Arun. But her realism has been defeated at the hand of the idealism of Nath, and Jyoti marries Arun. After the marriage, Nath understands the grave mistake of his life to push his daughter to lead a life based on his idealism, and his idealistic views of life are responsible for the wretched condition of his daughter. Jyoti, from her childhood, has been living under the impact of his father, and she has been taught never to give up in life, whatever the situation is. She has learnt to live like a soldier. At the end of the play, she clarifies that she will live with Arun and never give up in life to live like a soldier.

Arrogance

Arrogance is found in the character of Arun. He is a Dalit, and from his childhood, he has received a wretched atmosphere of life. It is Jyoti who sympathises with him and decides to marry him. For his sake, Jyoti has left her comfortable life. But Arun is an arrogant man, and he can't determine the sacrifice of Jyoti for him. After the marriage, he has destroyed her life, and he kicks and beats her. He becomes a successful author after the publication of his autobiography and probably may win the prestigious Sahitya Akademy Award, but he is too proud to forget how to talk with elders. He has printed the name of Nath, his father-in-law, in the posters and invitations for the programme in honour of his success without Nath's concern. Arun is educated, successful as an eminent figure in Marathi literature, but he is proud and arrogant.

Violence Creates Violence

In this play, Vijay Tendulkar has pointed out that violence creates violence. He uses a simile from world history. During the Second World War, Hitler did a massacre for the Jews and was violent for them, and after the World War, the Jews have established their own country, Israel, and now they do massacres for Palestine and its people. Here Tendulkar attempts to say that the Jews were once dominated and killed, and now they are dominating and killing. Such a situation has also been pointed out for the Indian class struggle. For generation after generation, the Dalit and subaltern people were tortured and dominated by the high caste; now Arun here takes revenge on the high caste society by torturing his wife, Jyoti, who belongs to the high caste.

Characters

Nath Devlalikar

He is the husband of Seva and father of Jyoti and Jayaprakash. He is an MLA, socialist, and activist for the Dalit culture and subaltern society. In the play, he has done the kanyadaan; he has given the hands of his daughter to Arun, who is a Dalit. Nath has an ideology to change society, and he has used his daughter as an experiment in this regard. But his experiment for the transformation of society is a failure. He is blind with his philosophy of life, and he pushes his daughter towards the suffering of life. Nath loves Arun before the marriage of his daughter, but this love has been transformed with hatred after the marriage. He, as a reader, praises the book of Arun, but as a father, he hates Arun and his book. He has to attend the programme reluctantly in honour of Arun and his book. Nath repents for his approval to the marriage of his daughter to Arun. Vijay Tendulkar has pointed out the agony of a father who has done kanyadaan in society through him.

Seva

Like her husband Nath, Seva is also an activist, and she works to develop women's welfare. She is not idealistic like her husband for marriage, and she thinks one woman should take enough time to judge a life partner before the final selection as there is no chance to mend it after the marriage. She has taken time to select Nath as a husband, and she criticises her daughter, Jyoti, for her hasty decision to take Arun as a partner. She does not approve of this marriage, whereas Nath approves this marriage. She is shocked to know that her daughter would assist her son-in-law in his brewing illicit liquor business. It is Seva who looks after her daughter after the marriage. She takes Jyoti to the nursing home for treatment when she is pregnant by six months. When Nath denies attending Arun's programme, she suggests Nath to attend the programme; otherwise, Arun will get a new excuse to beat their daughter.

Jyoti

Jyoti is the daughter of Nath and Seva. She is loved by her parents. She has married Arun, a Dalit, with the approval of Nath and the disapproval of Seva. Jyoti has been brought up under the impact of her father, and she has made a grave mistake in life that destroyed her life and grabs the harmony of her family. After her marriage, all the ideologies of Jyoti are pissed up by the reality of life. She has been beaten and kicked up by her husband, Arun, even though she is pregnant. She leaves her husband's house, but she returns. At the end of the play, she asks her parents not to communicate with her as she now belongs to her husband.

Arun

Arun is a Dalit, and he has married Jyoti, who has been infatuated with him through his poetry and autobiographical writing. He is a successful Dalit writer and probably may win the prestigious Sahitya Akademi Award for his autobiography. He is educated, but he is a beast and idler. He beats his wife and kicks her. He lives on the earning of Jyoti and drinks and beats her; Arun does not like his in-laws. He is arrogant and proud; he has printed the name of his father-in-law in the posters and invitations without the permission of Nath. He emotionally blackmails Nath to attend and deliver a speech in the programme in favour of his book. Arun may be an eccentric character who is not grateful at the morality of his wife and his well-wishers.

Jayaprakash

Jayaprakash is the son of Nath and Seva. He does his MSc. Like his mother, he does not approve of the relation of Jyoti with Arun. Throughout the play, he is noticed to serve teas to the other members of the family, especially Nath. He uses the simile of Israel and Palestine for the rude character of Arun for his sister, Jyoti. He thinks that once the ancestors of Arun were tormented by their ancestors and it is time for Arun to take revenge for it by tormenting Jyoti.

Bibliography

Bhave,Pushpa, Vijay Tendulkar: *A Study in Contemporary Indian Theatre*, Sangit Natak Akademi, New Delhi, 1989.

Dharan, N.S. *The Plays of Vijay Tendulkar*, Creative Books, New Delhi, 1999.

M. Sarat Babu, *Vijay Tendulkar's Ghashiram Kotwal: A Reader's Companion*, Asia Book Club, New Delhi, 2003.

Madge, V.M., *Vijay Tendulkar's Plays: An Anthology of Recent Criticism*, Delhi: Pencraft International, 2007.

Prasad, Amar Nath and Satish Barbuddhe, *The Plays of Vijay Tendulkar:* Critical Explorations, New Delhi: Sarup & Sons, 2008.

Tendulkar, *Vijay – Collected Plays in Translation*, Oxford University Press, 2003.

Wadikar, Shailaja B. *Vijay Tendulkar: A Pioneer Playwright*, New Delhi: Atlantic Publishers, 2008.

Index